Street by Street

REIGATE, F
DORKING
HORLEY, LEATHERHEAD
Ashtead, Bletchingley, Brockham, Fetcham,
Great Bookham, Kingswood, Merstham, Salfords,
South Nutfield, Tadworth, Walton on the Hill, Westcott

1st edition September 2002

© Automobile Association Developments
Limited 2002

oS Ordnance Survey® This product includes map
data licensed from Ordnance
Survey® with the permission
of the Controller of Her Majesty's Stationery Office.
© Crown copyright 2002. All rights reserved.
Licence No: 399221.

Published by AA Publishing (a trading name of
Automobile Association Developments
Limited, whose registered office is Millstream,
Maidenhead Road, Windsor, Berkshire SL4 5GD.
Registered number 1878835).

The Post Office is a registered trademark of Post
Office Ltd. in the UK and other countries.

Schools address data provided by Education Direct.

One-way street data provided by:

Tele Atlas © Tele Atlas N.V.

Mapping produced by the Cartographic
Department of The Automobile Association. A01100

A CIP Catalogue record for this book is
available from the British Library.

Printed by GRAFIASA S.A., Porto, Portugal

Ref: ML166

Key to map pages	ii-iii
Key to map symbols	iv-1
Street by Street	2-57
Index – towns & villages	58
Index – streets	59-66
Index – featured places	66-67

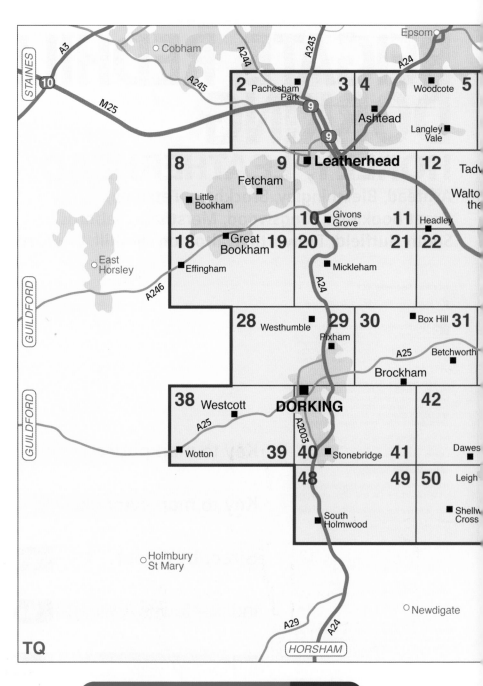

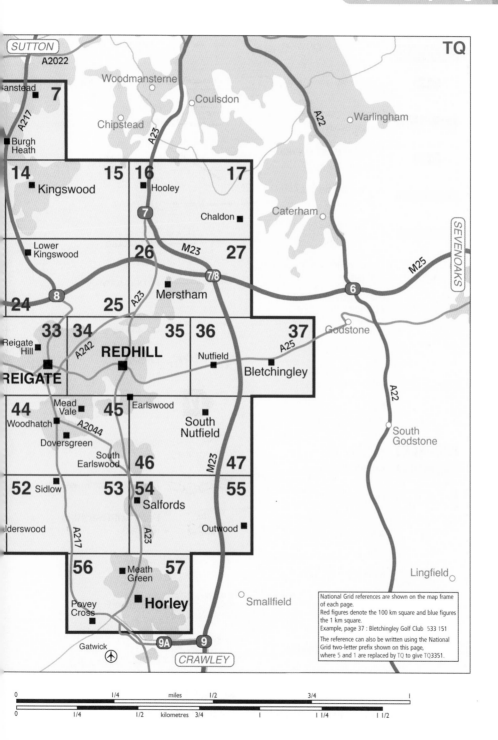

TQ

SUTTON
A2022

Woodmansterne

Coulsdon

anstead **7**

Chipstead

Warlingham

Burgh
Heath

A217

A23

A22

SEVENOAKS

14 **15** **16** **17**

Kingswood Hooley

Chaldon

Caterham

7

Lower
Kingswood **26** M23 **27**

M25

24 **8** **25** A23 Merstham **7/8** **6**

Godstone

33 **34** **35** **36** **37**

Reigate
Hill

A242

REDHILL Nutfield A25

Bletchingley

REIGATE

A22

44 Mead
Vale **45** Earlswood

Woodhatch A2044 South
Nutfield

Doversgreen

South
Godstone

South
Earlswood **46** M23 **47**

52 Sidlow **53** **54** **55**

Salfords

lderswood A217 A23 Outwood

Lingfield

56 **57**

Meath
Green

Smallfield

Povey
Cross **Horley**

Gatwick

9A **9**

CRAWLEY

National Grid references are shown on the map frame
of each page.
Red figures denote the 100 km square and blue figures
the 1 km square.
Example, page 37 : Bletchingley Golf Club 533 151

The reference can also be written using the National
Grid two-letter prefix shown on this page,
where 5 and 1 are replaced by TQ to give TQ3351.

0   1/4   miles   1/2   3/4   I
0   1/4   1/2   kilometres   3/4   I   I 1/4   I 1/2

iv

Junction 9	Motorway & junction	⊖	Underground station
Services	Motorway service area	⊖	Light railway & station
	Primary road single/dual carriageway	+++++++++	Preserved private railway
Services	Primary road service area	LC	Level crossing
	A road single/dual carriageway	•—•—•—•	Tramway
	B road single/dual carriageway	-----------	Ferry route
	Other road single/dual carriageway	....	Airport runway
	Minor/private road, access may be restricted	— · — · — · —	County, administrative boundary
← ←	One-way street	▼▼▼▼▼▼▼▼▼	Mounds
	Pedestrian area	17	Page continuation
============	Track or footpath		River/canal, lake, pier
	Road under construction		Aqueduct, lock, weir
⌐ - - - - ⌐	Road tunnel	465 ▲ Winter Hill	Peak (with height in metres)
AA	AA Service Centre		Beach
P	Parking		Woodland
P+🚌	Park & Ride		Park
🚌	Bus/coach station		Cemetery
	Railway & main railway station		Built-up area
	Railway & minor railway station		

Symbol	Description	Symbol	Description
	Featured building		Abbey, cathedral or priory
	City wall		Castle
A&E	Hospital with 24-hour A&E department		Historic house or building
PO	Post Office	Wakehurst Place NT	National Trust property
	Public library	M	Museum or art gallery
i	Tourist Information Centre		Roman antiquity
	Petrol station — Major suppliers only		Ancient site, battlefield or monument
†	Church/chapel		Industrial interest
	Public toilets		Garden
	Toilet with disabled facilities		Arboretum
PH	Public house — AA recommended		Farm or animal centre
	Restaurant — AA inspected		Zoological or wildlife collection
	Theatre or performing arts centre		Bird collection
	Cinema		Nature reserve
	Golf course	V	Visitor or heritage centre
▲	Camping — AA inspected		Country park
	Caravan Site — AA inspected		Cave
	Camping & caravan site — AA inspected		Windmill
	Theme park		Distillery, brewery or vineyard

2

A   B   C   D

514   15

Falconhurst

LEATHERHEAD ROAD

Charlwood Drive

Honeycroft

The

Burn Cl

Manor Way

ick Close

A244

Oaklawn Road

OXSHOTT

1

59

Manor Way

Tyrwhitt House

2

LANE   A245

Hotel

Woodlands Park

Dorincourt

M25

Oaklawn Road

WOODLANDS ROAD

Pachesham Park Golf Centre

3

58

Golf Course

KT22

4

A245

The Mounts

Kelvin A

Falcon Wood

5

57

Lane

River

RANDALLS

Cemetery

ROAD

514   15

A   B   **9**   C   D

Randalls Park

Cobham Road

aller Lane

Emerton Road

River La Mole Road

Friars Orch

Monks Grn

Sports Club

Cannon Way

LEATHERHE

1 grid square represents 500 metres

Epsom
Ewell & St Hellier
NHS Trust

Hotel

E **F** **G** **H**

21 22

I

Golf Course

Green Road

Chantry Hurst

Hylands Rise

Diggens Rise

Park Road

Woodside
Chalk Paddock Pixley

Chalk Place End

Woodcote
Hambledon Vale

Hambledon Hill

Axwood

Cedar Hill

Chalk La

The Durdans

Oak Hill

Pine Hill

Sunny Bank

Baron's
Hurst

Warren Hill

Woodcote

B290

Ridings

Milburn Wk

Treadwell Road

Walnut Cl

Hilcrest Cl

Aston Wy

Wootton Cl

Downs Way

Downs Way

Treadwell
Rd

Council
Building

Epsom
Cemetery

B289

BURGH

Beech Wy

B284

Carton

HEATH ROAD

59

2

Derby Stables
Road

Derby Arms
Rd

Grand Stand

Chalk Lane

ROAD

DOWNS

ROAD

ASHLEY ROAD
B290

Grandstand

TATTENHAM CORNER ROAD

Woodcote
Park

Barn Road

Ridge

Chalk Pit Road

Langley Vale Road

Epsom
Downs

3 Epsom Downs
Racecourse

58

6

4

Millers
Copse

Langley Cl

Saddlers
Way

Strand Cl

The Hayes

Mannamead

Roseberry
Road

Vale
Primary
School

Harding Rd

Grosvenor Road

Beaconsfield Road

Spencer Close

**Langley
Vale**

Walton
Downs

5

E **F** **G** **H**

21 22

57

KT18

12

Nohome
Farm

Ebbisham

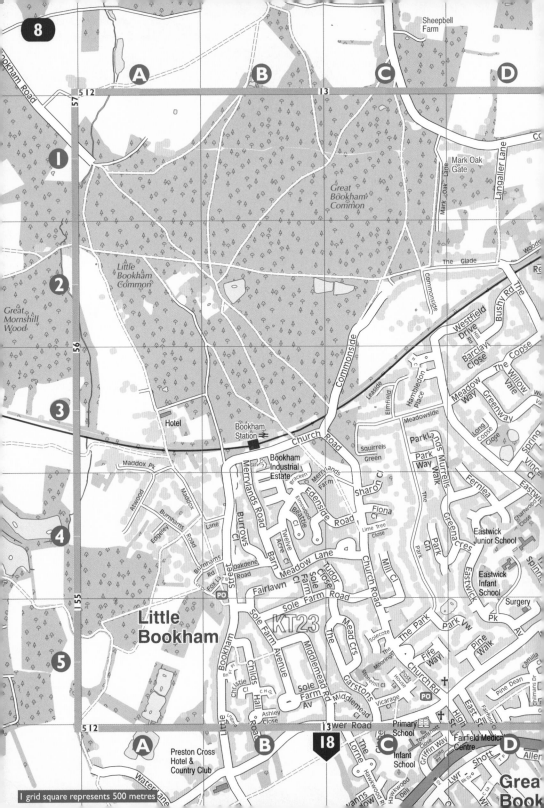

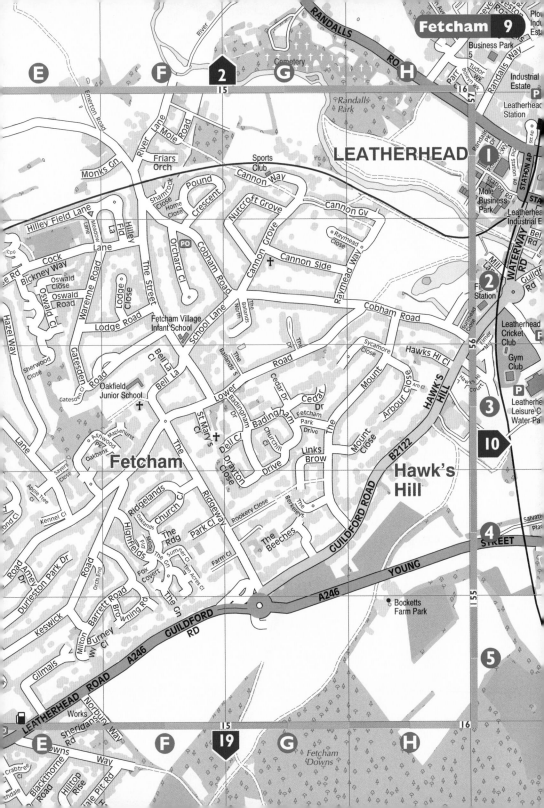

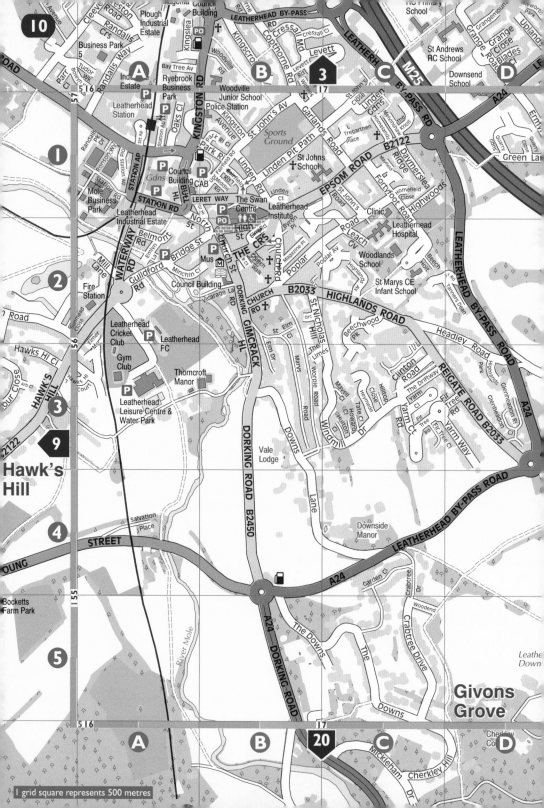

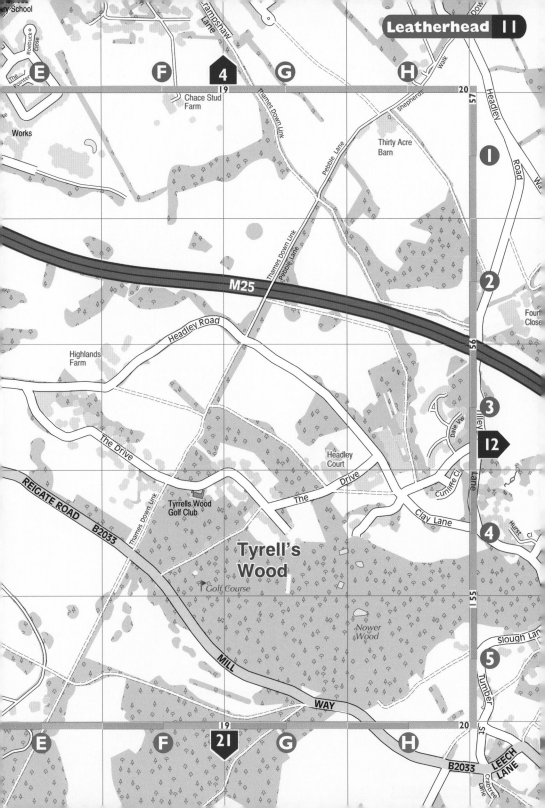

Chipstead Bottom

OUTWOOD L

E   F   G   H

27   28   57

Larch
Close

B2032

Castle

Road

Chipstead
RFC

Elmore

Road

I

Sta

Lane

2

Eyhurst
Farm

High Road

Hogscross

Noke Farm

56

Eyhurst
Court

3

16

White Hill

4

Pigeonhouse Lane

Southerns Lane

Reeves
Rest

High Road

Markedge Lane

55

swell

Rectory Road

Park
Farm

5

Harps

Oak

Fair

Lane

Boars Gr
Farm

27   28

E   F   25   G   H

Lane

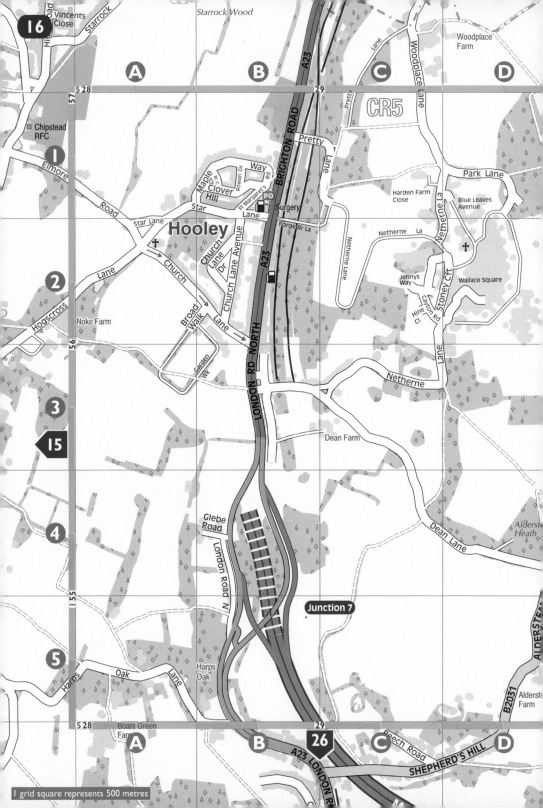

Coulsdon Common

Ellis Road

Goodenough Way

Weston

Middle Goodenough

Goodenough Cl

Lacy Cl

Lacey Dr

field

Tennison Cl

Commonside

d Av

COULSDON ROAD

Parson's Cle

Rugby Club

High School

Stites

Hill

Coulsdon

B2030

PH

Fox Cl

Plo

CV

I

The

London Loop

Hawarden Rd

Green Lane

Gownie Pl

Grenadier Pl

Bridge Place

Wellin

Magazine

Road

2

The Gullet

Cornwallis Cl

Croydon Surrey County

Golf Course

Happy Valley Golf Club

3

Court Farm

Leazes Avenue

Church Lane

Doctors Lane

Lane

LANE

4

Linden Dr

Mount Avenue

Chaldon

DEAN LANE

ROOK

B2031

Willey Broom La

St Peter & St Paul CE Primary School

Rook Farm

Lane

Birchcroft Close

Tollsworth Manor

Birchwood

5

Six Brothers Field

Pilgrims' Lane

owns Way

Gilmals

Milton Cl

Burney Cl

A246

LEATHERHEAD ROAD

Works

Sheridans Rd

Norbury Way

Downs

Crabtree Cl

Blackthorne Road

Hilltop Rise

Hale Pit Rd

Hales Oak

Crabtree Lane

rd Road

Downs Way

Downs VW Rd

Timber Close

Close

South Bookham School

Fetcham Downs

Norbury Park

Druids Grove

Chapel Lane

Phoenice Farm

Crabtree Cottage

Crabtree Lane

Chapel Farm

Bagden Farm

Chapel Lane

Westhu

E F **9** G H

I

2

3

20

4

5

E F **28** G H

15 16

54 53 152

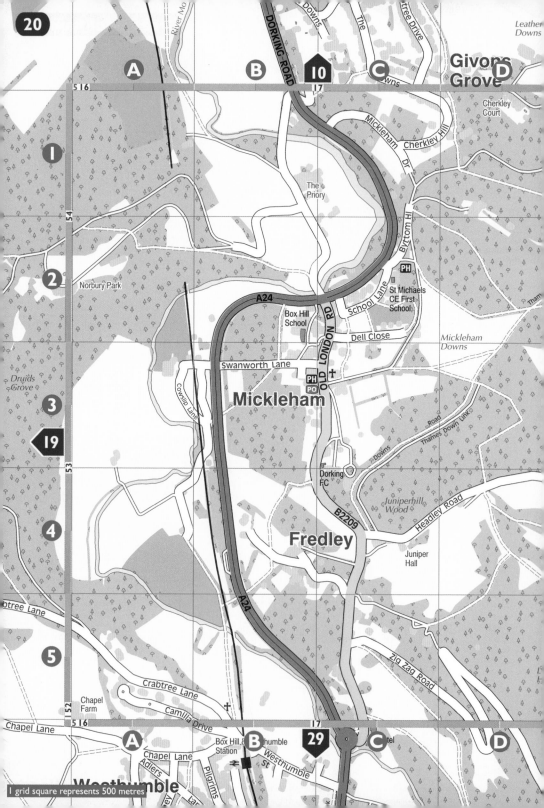

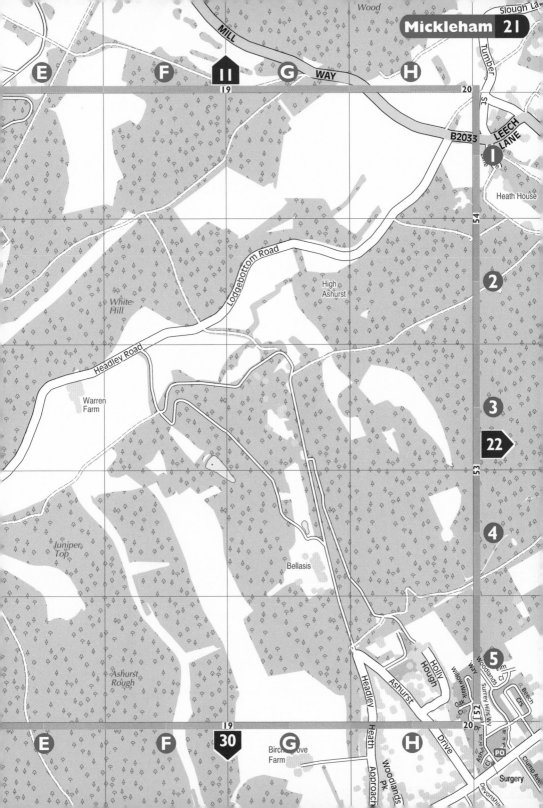

Wood

Slough La

MILL

WAY

E

F

II

G

H

Tumber

B2033

I

**LEECH
LANE**

St

Heath House

54

Lodgebottom Road

High
Ashurst

2

White
Hill

Headley Road

3

Warren
Farm

22

4

Juniper
Top

Bellasis

Holly
Hough

5

Ashurst
Rough

Headley

Ashurst

Willow Walk

Oak Cl

Woodlands

Surrey Hills Wy

Elm Cl

Beech

52

Way

Drs

E

F

30

G

Birchgrove
Farm

H

Heath

Drive

PO

Woodlands
PK

Devonshi

Approach

Surgery

E

F

13

G

H

CHEQUERS LANE

Walton on the Hill
CE Junior School

Chequers
Close

Nursery
Close

Holmcroft

Deans

Egmont Pk

Greenways

Russell Ct

Walton Heath
Golf Club

B2220

Wonford Cl

Hurst

Heath Drive

DORKING ROAD

B2032

Nyefield
Park

23

24

I

54

Golf Course

Banstead
Heath

2

Walton
Heath

The
Hermitage

3

24

ogador R

53

Grove

Mogador

Margery

4

M25

North Downs Way

Merrywood Grove

North Downs Way

5

52

Buckland

Lane

North Downs Way

23

32

erhill

24

E

F

G

H

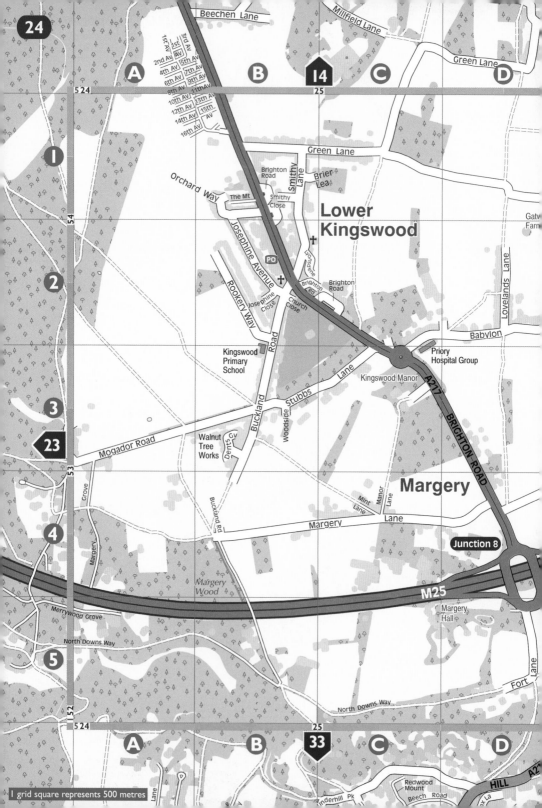

Beechen Lane
Millfield Lane
Green Lane

1st AV
2nd Av
3rd Av
4th Av
5th Av
6th Av
7th Av
8th Av
9th Av
10th Av
11th Av
12th Av
13th Av
14th Av
15th Av
16th Av

A
B
14
C
D

S 24
25

I

S 4

Orchard Way

Green Lane

Smithy Lane
Brighton Road

Brier Lea

The Mt
Smithy Close

Lower
Kingswood

2

Josephine Avenue

PO

Lyonsdene

Brighton Rd

Brighton Road

Gatw
Farm

Lovelands Lane

Rookery Way

Josephine Close

Church Close

Babylon

Priory
Hospital Group

Kingswood
Primary
School

Lane

Kingswood Manor

A217

3

Buckland Road

Stubbs

Woodside

Lane

BRIGHTON ROAD

23

S 3

Mogador Road

Walnut
Tree
Works

Dent's Gv

Margery

Grove

Mint
Lane

Manor
Lane

Buckland Rd

Margery   Lane

Junction 8

4

Margery
Wood

M25

Margery
Hall

Merrywood Grove

North Downs Way

Fort Lane

5

S 2

North Downs Way

S 24
25

A
B
33
C
D

Redwood
Mount

HILL

A2

Underhill Pk
Beech Road

k La

1 grid square represents 500 metres

swell

Rectory Road

Park Farm

E

F

15

G

H

I

27

28

Oak

Harps

Boars G Farm

Fair

Lane

Lane

Markedge Lane

54

Upper Gatton Park

2

Old Mint House

Crossways Farm

M25

Gatton Bottom

Whitehall Farm

Crossways

Lane

Lane

3

Reigate Golf Clu

26

53

Gatton

N Downs Wy

The Royal Alexandra & Albert School

Gatton Hall

N Downs Way

4

North Downs Way

E-HILL

ns Way

The Lake

5

Wray Lane

152

E

F

34

G

ROAD

H

PO

Ringwood Av

DON ROAD

27

PARK

North Md

Monson

Lyndale Road

Clare Rd

Ranmore Close

Holc court

St Bede's School

Colesmead

Works

Alpi Roa

Gatton

Gatton

Carlton Green

Coles

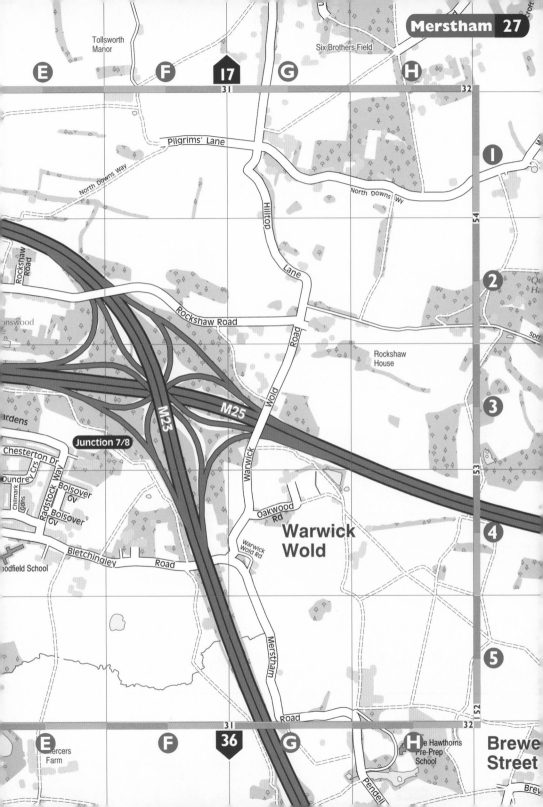

E   F   **17**   G   H
31   32

Tollsworth Manor

Six Brothers Field

croft

I
54

Pilgrims' Lane

North Downs Way

North Downs Wy

2

Rockshaw Road

Hilltop Lane

Rockshaw Road

Q
Ha

Sprl

onswood

Rockshaw House

Wold Road

3

M23

M25

Junction 7/8

Chesterton Dr

Lilacs Crs

Dundre

Chilmark Gdns

Radstock Way

Bolsover Gv

Bolsover Gv

ardens

Warwick

Warwick Wold Rd

Oakwood Rd

Warwick Wold

53

4

Bletchingley   Road

odfield School

Mercers Farm

Merstham

5
52

E   F   **36**   G   H
31   32

Road

e Hawthorns Pre-Prep School

**Brewe
Street**

Pendell

Bre

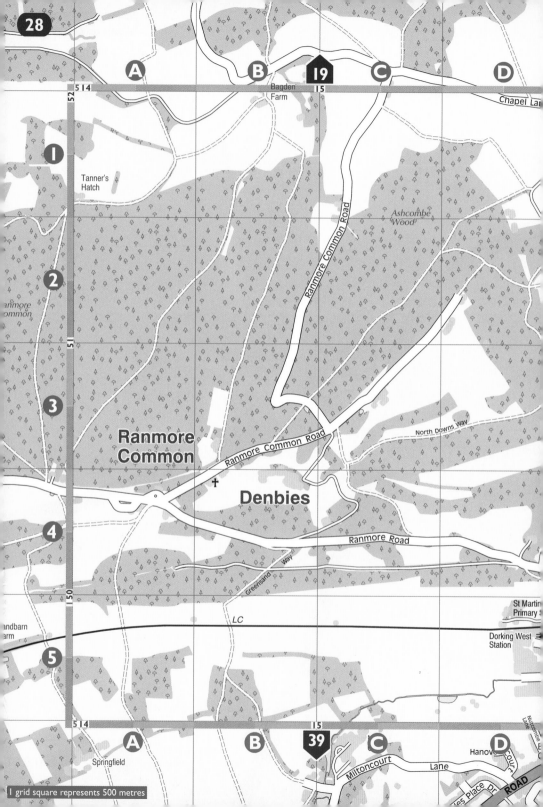

28

A   B   **19**   C   D

52 14   Bagden   15   Chapel Lan
Farm

I

Tanner's
Hatch

Ashcombe
Wood

Ranmore Common Road

2

51

anmore
ommon

3

**Ranmore
Common**

North Downs Way

Ranmore Common Road

†

Denbies

4

Ranmore Road

Greensand Way

50

St Martin
Primary

LC

Dorking West
Station

5

andbarn
arm

514

A   B   **39**   C   D

15

Springfield   Miltoncourt   Hanove
Lane   ROAD

1 grid square represents 500 metres

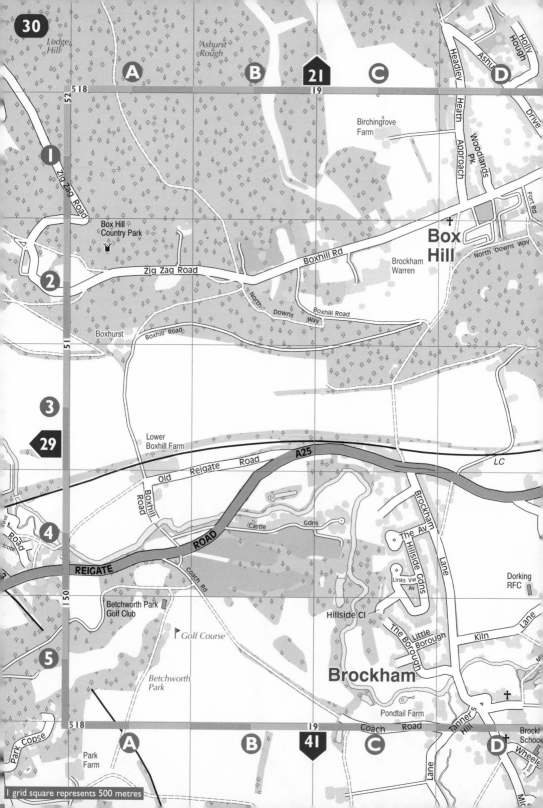

30

A   B   **21**   C   D

Lodge Hill

Ashurst Rough

Holly Hough

Ashu

Headley Heath

Woodlands Pk

Birchingrove Farm

Drive

Fort Rd

52 | 518

19

1

Zig Zag Road

Box Hill Country Park

Box Hill

North Downs Way

Brockham Warren

Approach

2

Zig Zag Road

North Downs Way

Boxhill Rd

Boxhill Road

51

Boxhurst

Boxhill Road

3

29

Lower Boxhill Farm

Old Reigate Road

A25

LC

Boxhill Road

4

Castle

Gdns

Brockham Lane

The Av

Hillside Gdns

Lane

Dorking RFC

REIGATE

ROAD

Coach Rd

Links Vw Av

150

Betchworth Park Golf Club

Golf Course

Hillside Cl

The Borough

Little Borough

Kiln Lane

Lane

5

Betchworth Park

Brockham

Tanner's Hill

Brockl School

Park Copse

Pondtail Farm

Coach Road

Wheel

518

19

A   B   **41**   C   D

Park Farm

Lane

Mi

1 grid square represents 500 metres

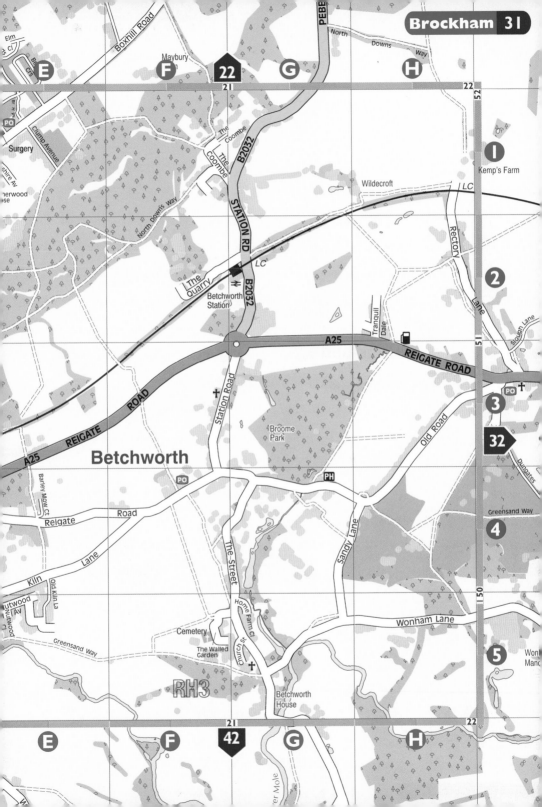

32

A   B   **23**   C   D

S 22

1

Kemp's Farm

LC

Rectory Lane

2

Slough Lane

Buckland

REIGATE ROAD

A25

PO †

3

Old Road

31

Dungates Lane

Greensand Way

4

Dungate's Farm

S 50

Wonham Lane

5

Wonham Manor

Trumpetshill

Trumpets Hill

Sandy Lane

North Downs Way

Underhill Farm

Dowde's Farm

Lawrence Lane

Clifton's Lane

Colle

A25   BUC

Reigate Heath

Golf Course

Reigate Heath Golf Club †

Flanchford

Bonnys Rd

Lane

Heathfield

Gree Way

A   B   **43**   C   D

S 22

Littleton

1 grid square represents 500 metres

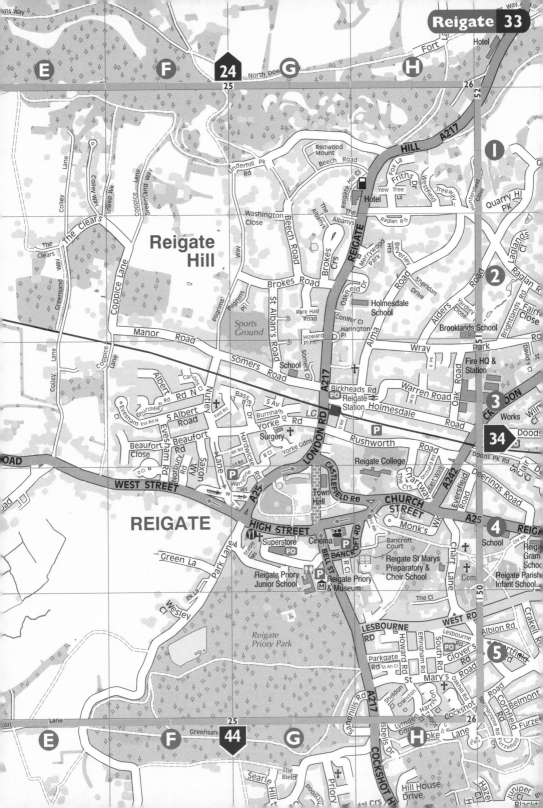

A   B   27   C   D

52   5 30   31   Road

Merstham

The Hawtho
Pre-Prep
School

Mercers
Farm

I

Marsh Road

Nutfield
Marsh

Nutfield

Marsh

Road

Pendell

Pendell
Road

...head
Lane

Chilmead Lane

2

51

Big Common Lane

Church Hill

3

CAST

BLETCHINGLEY RD   A25

Blacklands
Meadow

Doods
Brow
School

Shortacres

Deans La

Cemetery

Park Works
Rd

Parkwood Rd

HIGH STREET

Cooper's
Hill

M23

A25

NUTFIELD ROAD

Nutfield

Greens...

4

Sandy Lane

Mid Street

Cooper's
Hill Road

50

5

Sandy Lane

Greensand Way

Braes Md

Bower Hill Lane

Kentwyns
Rise

Nutfield Church CE
Primary School

Lyttel
Hall

Greensand Way

5 30   31

South
Nutfield

A   B   47   C   D

Trindles Road

Mid Street

Nutfield
...on

PO

Holmesdale
Road

Greensand

1 grid square represents 500 metres

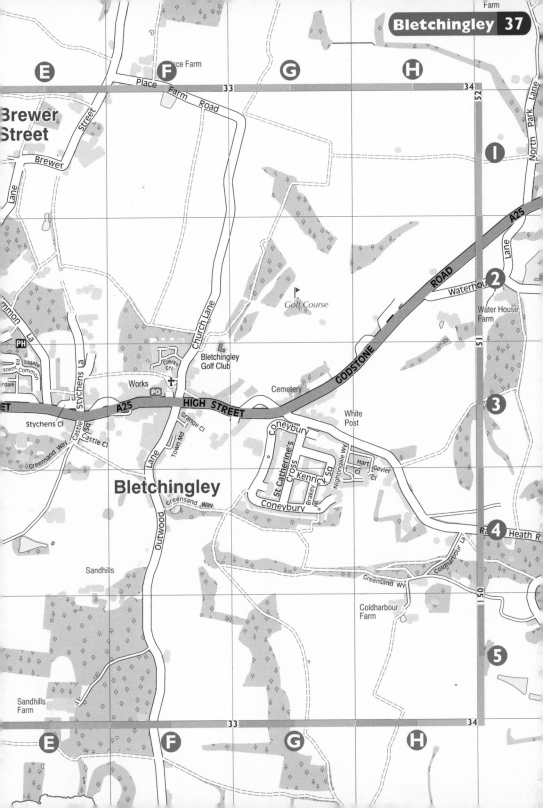

E
F
Place Farm
G
H

Place
Farm
Road
33
34
52

**Brewer
Street**

Street

Brewer
Lane

I

A25

North Park Lane

Lane

PH
Common La

Golf Course

Church Lane

Waterhou
2

Water House
Farm

Bletchingley
Golf Club

GODSTONE

ROAD

51

Stychens La

Clerk's
Cft

Works
PO

Cemetery

3

Tilgate
common
scent
rdale
Rd

HIGH STREET

A25

White
Post

Stychens Cl

Castle Sq
Castle Cl

Grange Cl

Town Md

Lane

Coneybury

Nightingale Wy

Hart
Cl

Gayler
Cl

Greensand Way

St Catherine's
Cross

Kenrick Sq

Bletchingley

Greensand Way

Coneybury

Brakey
Hil

Ra
4
Heath R

Coldharbour La

Outwood

Greensand Wy

150

Sandhills

Coldharbour
Farm

5

Sandhills
Farm

E
F
G
H
33
34

38

White Downs

Nor**A** Downs Way **B** **C** **D**

512 13

1

49

Rokefield

Hole Hill Lane

Surg

2

Stockman's Coomb Farm

Balchins Lane

Deerleap Road

West

Sandrock Road

Park Farm

Vale Farm

Coast Hill Lane

A25

Greensand Way

3

48

COAST HILL

Rookery Drive

The Rookery

Westcott Heath

West Lane

4

COAST HILL

Wotton

A25

Sheephouse Lane

Sheephouse Green

Wolvens Lane

5

Ma Fa

Wotton Drive

Greensand Way

47

Wotton House

512 13

A **B** **C** **D** Log Gre

Hollow La

I grid square represents 500 metres

RH4

Westcott

Springfield

Milton Court

Hanover Court

Bowling Club

The Dorking Business Park

Curtis Close

Beech Cl

Miltoncourt Lane

WESTCOTT ROAD

A25

STATION RD

Industrial Estate

Primary School

Sondes Place Dr

Road Glebe

Nower Road

Howard Rd

Vincent Lane

Vincent Drive

The Priory School

Powell Corderoy Primary School

Longfield Rd School

Longfield Rd

West Bank

Nower Lodge School

Lince Lane

Milton Heath

Hampstead

Greensand Way

The Nower

Home Farm

Columbour Lane

Ridge Cl

Kr

Hildens

Milton Street

Westlees Farm

Chadhurst Farm

House

Parsonage Road

Institute Road

St John's Rd

Ashley Road

Watson Road

Bailey Road

The Burrell

Chapel La

Stones Lane

Pointer's Hill

Broomfield Pk

First School

School La

Milton Av

Furlong Road

PO

ROAD A25

FORD

28

E F G H

I

2

3

40

4

5

E F G H

15 16

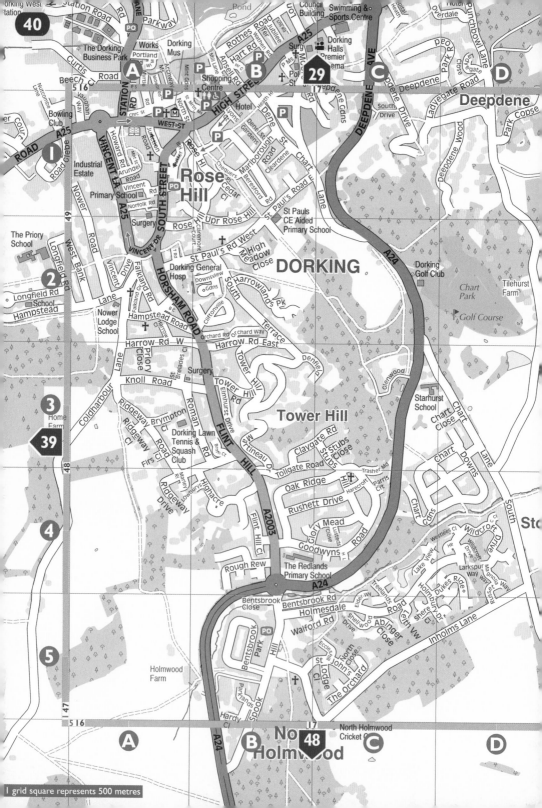

I grid square represents 500 metres

Golf Course

Little Borough

Kiln

Brockham

Betchworth Park

E **F** **30** **G** Pondtail Farm

Coach Road

Tanner's Hill

H †

Brockham School

Wheelers La

Dodds Pk

1

Wheelers

Oak

Oakdene Rd

Park Farm

Terrenne Road

49

School Lane

Middle Street

20

Moat House Farm

2

Glenfield Road

Glenfield Close

Brew House

Silverdale Close

Tanners Meadow

Surgery

3

Tanner's Brook

Lane

Boxhill Way

Tynedale

Tynedale Cl

Ridge Cl

42

lee Terrace

Tilehurst Lane

Felton's Farm

Lands

Tweed Lane

Ridge Cl

Park Cl

48

4

Parkpale Lane

Bushbury Lane

Bushbury

Coleshill Farm

idge

Roothill

5

Roothill

147

20

E **F** **19** **49** **G** Great Brockhamhurst **H** Road

La

Brockhamhu

Blackbrook

PH

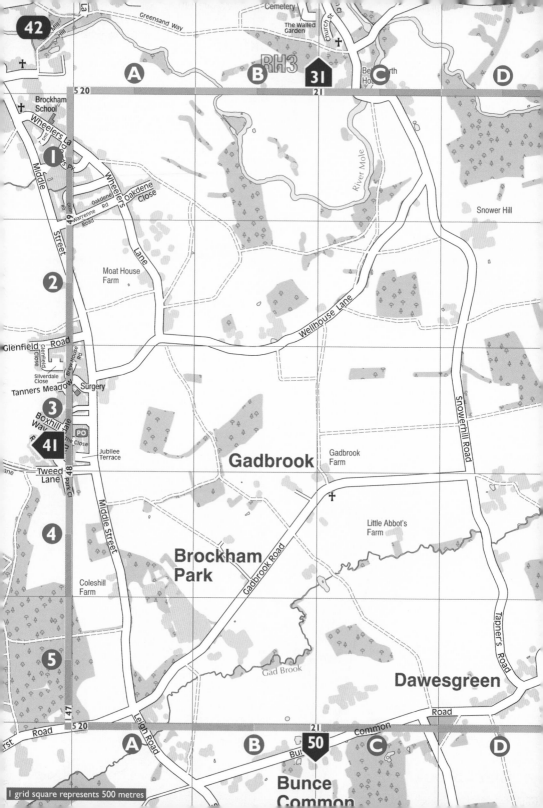

E
Wonham
Manor

Trumpetshill

Sandy
Lane

F

32
Trumpets Hill
23

G
Heathfield

H

Littleton

24

I

49

Littleton
Manor Farm

Flanchford Road

Santon
House

Wallace
Brook

2
Clayhall Lane

Ricebridge Farm

Flanchford
Farm

3

44

Little
Flanchford

Flanchford Road

48

4

River Mole

Leigh
Place

Burys Court
School

5

Leigh Place Road

147

PO E PH

F

51

G

H

24

Harrington
Close

Bures
Manor

eigh

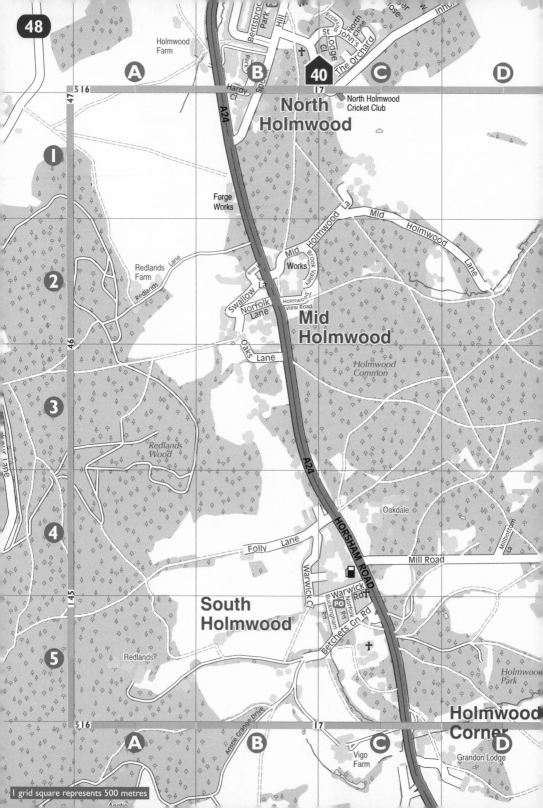

E   F   **41**   G   H

Blackbrook

PH

Blackbrook Road

Roothill Lane

Great Brockhamhurst

Brockhamhurst Road

Red Lane

I

Wes Con

2

Brook Lodge Farm

3

Lodge Farm

50

Lane

Lodge

Hawesrew Farm

4

Henfold Lane

Brookside

5

Ewood Farm

Ewoo

Petersfield Farm

Ewood Lane

Swires Farm

E   F   G   H

19   20   47   46   45

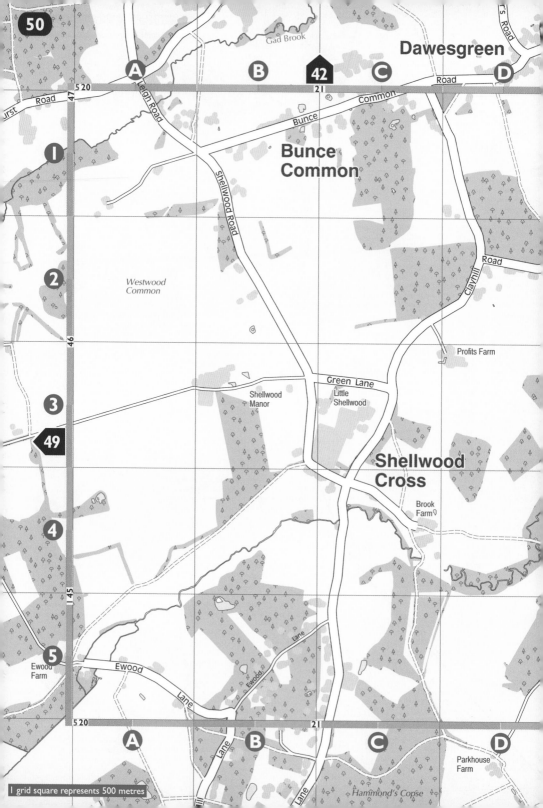

50

Dawesgreen

(A) 5 20 47

Hurst Road

Leigh Road

(B)

Gad Brook

42 21

(C)

Road

(D)

Bunce Common

**Bunce
Common**

1

Shellwood Road

2

*Westwood
Common*

Clayhill Road

Profits Farm

Green Lane

3

*Shellwood
Manor*

Little
Shellwood

49

**Shellwood
Cross**

Brook
Farm

4

145

5

Ewood
Farm

Ewood

Lane

Ewood

Lane

Lane

5 20

(A)

(B) 21

(C)

(D)

Parkhouse
Farm

Hammond's Copse

I grid square represents 500 metres

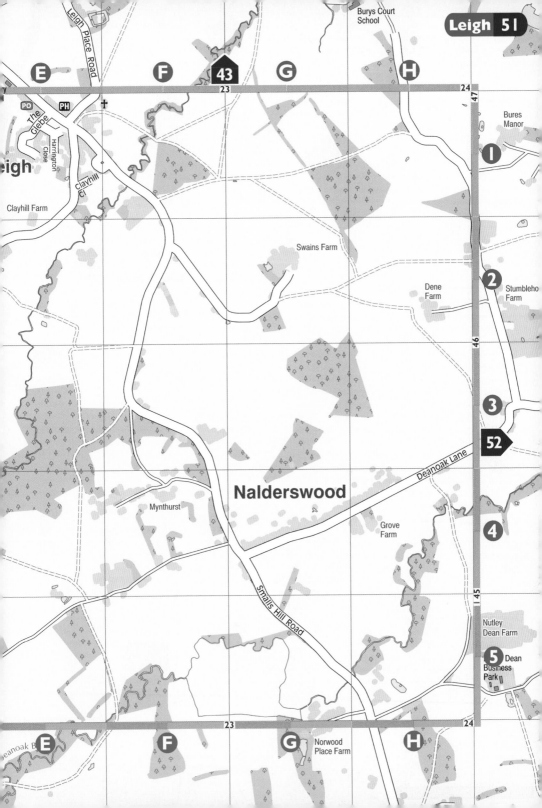

Leigh Place Road

Burys Court School

E
F
43
G
H

23
24

47

PO
PH
The Glebe
Harrington Close

Bures Manor

I

eigh

Clayhill Cl

Clayhill Farm

Swains Farm

Dene Farm

Stumbleho Farm

2

46

3

52

Deanoak Lane

Nalderswood

Mynthurst

Grove Farm

4

45

Smalls Hill Road

Nutley Dean Farm

5 Dean Business Park

eanoak B

E
F
G
Norwood Place Farm
H

23
24

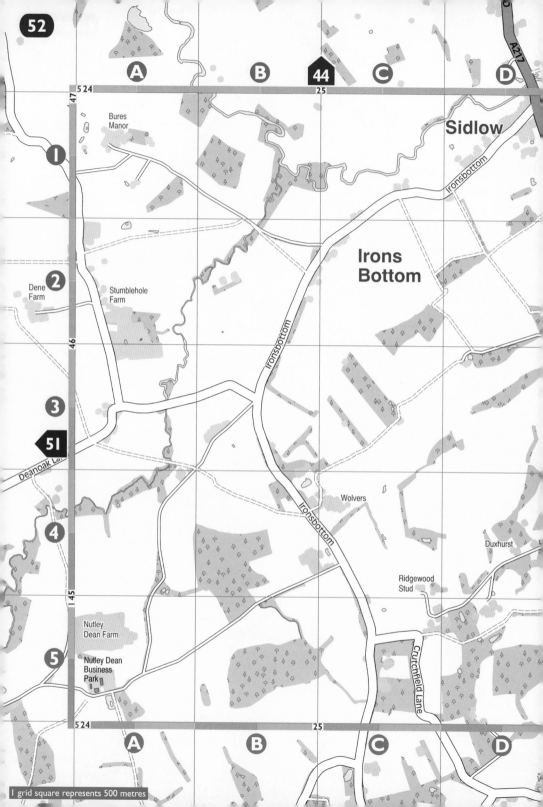

52

A   B   **44**   C   D

5 24   47   25

1

Bures
Manor

Sidlow

Ironsbottom

**Irons
Bottom**

2
Dene
Farm

Stumblehole
Farm

Ironsbottom

3

51

Deanoak La.

Wolvers

4

Duxhurst

Ironsbottom

Ridgewood
Stud

Nutley
Dean Farm

5
Nutley Dean
Business
Park

Crutchfield Lane

5 24   25

A   B   C   D

46

1 45

A217

1 grid square represents 500 metres

E

F

45
27

G

H
Brooks
Farm

28

47

Copsleigh
Way

Copsleigh
Salford
Prim Sch

Copsleigh Avenue

I

Hotel
PO

✝

Lonesome Lane

Lonesome
Farm

Park View Rd

Park Av

Brighton Rd

2

Kinnersley
Manor

Lodge Lane

Bmnts

Montfort Rise

Oak Lodge
Dr

46

Horley Ldg La

Wood
Cl

Fontigarry Farm
Business
Park

Horley
Lodge

Harwood
Park

3

Meath Green Lane

54

Ladyland Farm

4

River Mole

145

5

REIGATE ROAD

E
ell

F

56
27

G

Bay Cl

Poynes Rd

Palmer

Road South

Way

28

Kingsley

H

Todds
Cl

Tarnam
Cl

Bolters

Kingsley
Av

Parklawn

Road

Avondale Cl

Bolters Rd

The Spinn

Meath

Park Cres

Greenfields Rd

Greenfields

Mosford
Cl

Way

Infant
School

Deepfields

Newlands

Mallard Cl

Hutch

Kingfi

Kin

Way

54

Woodside Way

West Avenue

Copsleigh Way

A

B

46

C

D

Salford Prim Sch

28

Copsleigh

Dean Farm

I

Park Av

47

Hotel
PO

Honeycrock

Lane

Lane

June Lane

Axeland Park

Axes

Lane

Brownslade

Mead

Southern Av

Westmead Drive

Brighton Rd

Salbrook Road

Perrywood Business Park

Avenue

New House

2

46

Oak Lodge Dr

Montfort Rise

Salfords Station

SALFORDS

Picketts

Bmnts

Horley Ldg La

Salfords Industrial Estate

Orchard Business Centre

Picketts Lane

3

Horley Lodge

Wood Cl

A23

Harwood Park

53

Salfords Industrial Est

4

Astra Business Centre

Heath Business Centre

Beechwood Villas

Empire Villas

Cross Oak Lane

5

BONEHURST ROAD

45

28

Burstow Stream

Litt
Fa

Road South

Way

Darenth Way

Kingsley Way

Parklawn Way

A

Avondale Cl

Bottels Rd

Spinney

A23

Skipton Way

Sarel Way

Lake Lane

B

57

Greatlake Farm

C

D

Infant School

Neva

Drive

Mallard

HORLEY

1 grid square represents 500 metres

E **F** **47** **G** **H**

I

2

3

4

5

Moats Lane

Lane

South Hale Farm

Hatch Lane

Green Lane

Shepheard's Hurst

Prince of Wales Road

Woolborough Lane

Orchard Farm

Dalseys Hill

Bellwether Lane

Bellwether La

Miller's Lane

Miller's Copse

Wasp Green Lane

Brickfield Road

Outwo

W G

Hathersham Farm

M23

Rookery Farm

Rookery Hill

Norman's

E **F** **G** **H**

56

A · B · 53 · C · D

5 26 · 27 · Bay Cl · Road South

The Dell · Poynes Rd · Todds · Palmer · Boiter · Kingsley
Farnam · Cl · Kingsley Av · Parkholm Way · New

1 · Kingsley · Mosford Cl · Hutchins Way
Wrays · Greenfields Rd · Deepfields
Crutchfield · Landen Park · Greenfields Cl · Junior
Farm · Arne Gv · Greenfields Rd · School · How

44 · Westleas · Meath Green Lane · St A
Chesters · Meath Gn · Charlesfie
Meath · Dene · Av · Wor
Green · Chaffinch Wy · Willow Bream · Orchard Cl

A127 · Charm · Cl · Road · Grove Road
Close · Wither Dl · PO · Wickham · Vicarage

2 · Goldcrest · Parkhurst · Bliff Cl · Street · Bremner Av · Priory Cl
Cl · Way · Mill Cl · Baden · Bayfield
Whitmore · Lee · Powell · Rd · Blundell
Cl · Emlyn Rd · Av · First
court · Rd · Ramsey · School
Lodge · Cl · Rutherwick · Manor
Roffey · Cl · Dr

3 · Gower Rd · Thornton Pl · Manor
43 · Lane · Drake Road · Cl · Ashleigh
Mill · Thornton · P · Sangers · Cl
Thornton · Sports · County · Sanger
Centre · Middle School
Cemetery
Nursery Lane · Church Rd
4 · River Mole · PH

Hookwood · A217 · Church
Superstore · Gatwick Park · WK · Oldfield
Kennel Lane · Reigate · Hospital · Hotel · Woodroyd · Rd
Sideways · Lane · Malcolm · Withey · Av · A23 · Wolverton
5 · Gdns · Meadows · Fire · Longbridge Road
Station · Lng Wk · West S
Road · Hotel · Hotel
Povey Cross · Povey · Cross · Road · North
42 · Perimeter · Road · Longbridge Rd
5 26 · 27 · Service Rd

A · B · C · Northgate · D
North · Arrivals · Hotel
Terminal · Departures · Service Rd
1 grid square represents 500 metres · Rd

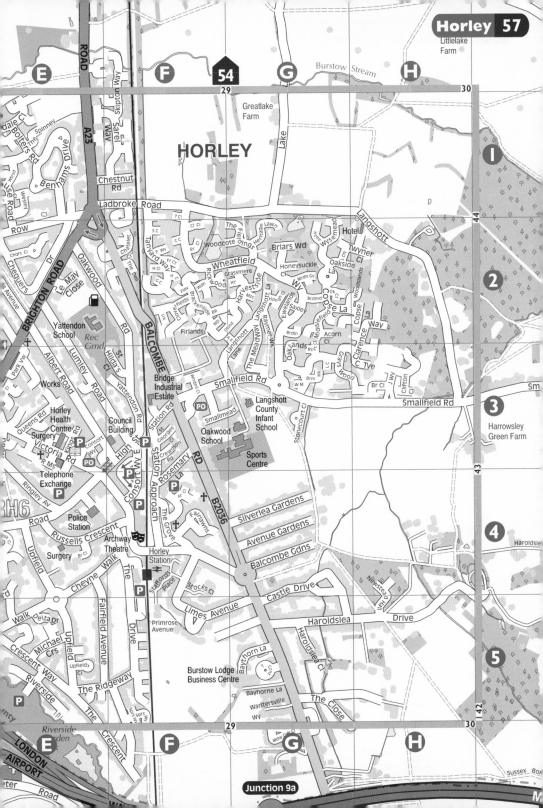

Ashtead 4 A3
Banstead 7 G1
Betchworth 31 E3
Blackbrook 49 E1
Bletchingley 37 F4
Box Hill 30 C2
Brewer Street 37 E1
Brockham 30 C5
Brockham Park 42 A4
Buckland 32 A3
Bunce Common 50 B1
Burgh Heath 6 D4
Bushbury 41 G4
Chaldon 17 H4
Coles Meads 34 D1
Dawesgreen 42 C5
Deepdene 40 D1
Denbies 28 B4
Dorking 40 B2
Doversgreen 44 D3
Earlswood 45 H1

Fetcham 9 F3
Fredley 20 B4
Gadbrook 42 B3
Gatton 25 H3
Givons Grove 10 D5
Great Bookham 18 D1
Hawk's Hill 9 H4
Headley 22 A1
Holmethorpe 35 F2
Holmwood Corner 48 D5
Hookwood 56 A4
Hooley 16 A2
Horley 57 F1
Irons Bottom 52 C2
Kingswood 14 B3
Langley Vale 5 F5
Leatherhead 9 G1
Leigh 51 E1
Little Bookham 8 A5
Lower Ashtead 3 G4
Lower Kingswood 24 C1

Margery 24 C4
Mead Vale 45 E2
Meath Green 56 B1
Merstham 26 B3
Mickleham 20 B3
Mid Holmwood 48 B2
Mogador 23 H4
Mugswell 14 D5
Naldersworth 51 G4
North Holmwood 48 B1
Nutfield 36 B4
Pachesham Park 3 E1
Pixham 29 G3
Povey Cross 56 A5
Ranmore Common 28 A3
Redhill 35 E2
Reigate 33 F4
Reigate Hill 33 F2
Ridge Green 47 E2
Rose Hill 40 A1
Salfords 54 B2

Shellwood Cross 50
Sidlow 52
South Earlswood 45
South Holmwood 48
South Merstham 26
South Nutfield 47
South Park 44
Stonebridge 40
Tadworth 13
Tower Hill 40
Tyrell's Wood 11
Walton on the Hill 12
Warwick Wold 27
Westcott 39
Westhumble 29
Whitebushes 46
Woodcote 5
Woodhatch 44
Wotton 38
Wray Common 34

USING THE STREET INDEX

Street names are listed alphabetically. Each street name is followed by its postal town or area locality, the Postcode District, the page number, and the reference to the square in which the name is found.

Standard index entries are shown as follows:

Abbotts Ri *REDH* RH1 ....**35** E2

Street names and selected addresses not shown on the map due to scale restrictions are shown in the index with an asterisk.

Albion Mews *REIG* * RH2.................**45** E1

GENERAL ABBREVIATIONS

ACC ....ACCESS	E ....EAST	LDG ....LODGE	R ....RIVE
ALY ....ALLEY	EMB ....EMBANKMENT	LGT ....LIGHT	RBT ....ROUNDABOU
AP ....APPROACH	EMBY ....EMBASSY	LK ....LOCK	RD ....ROA
AR ....ARCADE	ESP ....ESPLANADE	LKS ....LAKES	RDG ....RIDG
ASS ....ASSOCIATION	EST ....ESTATE	LNDG ....LANDING	REP ....REPUBLI
AV ....AVENUE	EX ....EXCHANGE	LTL ....LITTLE	RES ....RESERVO
BCH ....BEACH	EXPY ....EXPRESSWAY	LWR ....LOWER	RFC ....RUGBY FOOTBALL CLU
BLDS ....BUILDINGS	EXT ....EXTENSION	MAG ....MAGISTRATE	RI ....RIS
BND ....BEND	F/O ....FLYOVER	MAN ....MANSIONS	RP ....RAM
BNK ....BANK	FC ....FOOTBALL CLUB	MD ....MEAD	RW ....ROW
BR ....BRIDGE	FK ....FORK	MDW ....MEADOWS	S ....SOUT
BRK ....BROOK	FLD ....FIELD	MEM ....MEMORIAL	SCH ....SCHOO
BTM ....BOTTOM	FLDS ....FIELDS	MKT ....MARKET	SE ....SOUTH EAS
BUS ....BUSINESS	FLS ....FALLS	MKTS ....MARKETS	SER ....SERVICE ARE
BVD ....BOULEVARD	FLS ....FLATS	ML ....MALL	SH ....SHOR
BY ....BYPASS	FM ....FARM	ML ....MILL	SHOP ....SHOPPIN
CATH ....CATHEDRAL	FT ....FORT	MNR ....MANOR	SKWY ....SKYWA
CEM ....CEMETERY	FWY ....FREEWAY	MS ....MEWS	SMT ....SUMMI
CEN ....CENTRE	FY ....FERRY	MSN ....MISSION	SOC ....SOCIET
CFT ....CROFT	GA ....GATE	MT ....MOUNT	SP ....SPU
CH ....CHURCH	GAL ....GALLERY	MTN ....MOUNTAIN	SPR ....SPRIN
CHA ....CHASE	GDN ....GARDEN	MTS ....MOUNTAINS	SQ ....SQUAR
CHYD ....CHURCHYARD	GDNS ....GARDENS	MUS ....MUSEUM	ST ....STREE
CIR ....CIRCLE	GLD ....GLADE	MWY ....MOTORWAY	STN ....STATIO
CIRC ....CIRCUS	GLN ....GLEN	N ....NORTH	STR ....STREA
CL ....CLOSE	GN ....GREEN	NE ....NORTH EAST	STRD ....STRAN
CLFS ....CLIFFS	GND ....GROUND	NW ....NORTH WEST	SW ....SOUTH WES
CMP ....CAMP	GRA ....GRANGE	O/P ....OVERPASS	TDG ....TRADIN
CNR ....CORNER	GRG ....GARAGE	OFF ....OFFICE	TER ....TERRAC
CO ....COUNTY	GT ....GREAT	ORCH ....ORCHARD	THWY ....THROUGHWA
COLL ....COLLEGE	GTWY ....GATEWAY	OV ....OVAL	TNL ....TUNNE
COM ....COMMON	GV ....GROVE	PAL ....PALACE	TOLL ....TOLLWA
COMM ....COMMISSION	HGR ....HIGHER	PAS ....PASSAGE	TPK ....TURNPIK
CON ....CONVENT	HL ....HILL	PAV ....PAVILION	TR ....TRAC
COT ....COTTAGE	HLS ....HILLS	PDE ....PARADE	TRL ....TRAI
COTS ....COTTAGES	HO ....HOUSE	PH ....PUBLIC HOUSE	TWR ....TOWE
CP ....CAPE	HOL ....HOLLOW	PK ....PARK	U/P ....UNDERPASS
CPS ....COPSE	HOSP ....HOSPITAL	PKWY ....PARKWAY	UNI ....UNIVERSIT
CR ....CREEK	HRB ....HARBOUR	PL ....PLACE	UPR ....UPPE
CREM ....CREMATORIUM	HTH ....HEATH	PLN ....PLAIN	V ....VAL
CRS ....CRESCENT	HTS ....HEIGHTS	PLNS ....PLAINS	VA ....VALLE
CSWY ....CAUSEWAY	HVN ....HAVEN	PLZ ....PLAZA	VIAD ....VIADUC
CT ....COURT	HWY ....HIGHWAY	POL ....POLICE STATION	VIL VILL
CTRL ....CENTRAL	IMP ....IMPERIAL	PR ....PRINCE	VIS ....VIST
CTS ....COURTS	IN ....INLET	PREC ....PRECINCT	VLG ....VILLAG
CTYD ....COURTYARD	IND EST ....INDUSTRIAL ESTATE	PREP ....PREPARATORY	VLS ....VILLAS
CUTT ....CUTTINGS	INF ....INFIRMARY	PRIM ....PRIMARY	VW ....VIEW
CV ....COVE	INFO ....INFORMATION	PROM ....PROMENADE	W ....WES
CYN ....CANYON	INT ....INTERCHANGE	PRS ....PRINCESS	WD ....WOO
DEPT ....DEPARTMENT	IS ....ISLAND	PRT ....PORT	WHF ....WHAR
DL ....DALE	JCT ....JUNCTION	PT ....POINT	WK ....WAL
DM ....DAM	JTY ....JETTY	PTH ....PATH	WKS ....WALKS
DR ....DRIVE	KG ....KING	PZ ....PIAZZA	WLS ....WELLS
DRO ....DROVE	KNL ....KNOLL	QD ....QUADRANT	WY ....YARD
DRY ....DRIVEWAY	L ....LAKE	QU ....QUEEN	YD ....YARD
DWGS ....DWELLINGS	LA ....LANE	QY ....QUAY	YHA ....YOUTH HOSTEL

OSTCODE TOWNS AND AREA ABBREVIATIONS

Index - streets

1st - Bur

A

Av KWD/TDW/WH KT20 .....14 A5
d Av KWD/TDW/WH KT20 .....14 A5
Av KWD/TDW/WH KT20 .....14 A5
Av KWD/TDW/WH KT20 .....14 A5
Av KWD/TDW/WH KT20 .....14 A5
Av KWD/TDW/WH KT20 .....24 A1
Av KWD/TDW/WH KT20 .....14 A5
Av KWD/TDW/WH KT20 .....24 A1
ch Av KWD/TDW/WH KT20 .....14 A5
ch Av KWD/TDW/WH KT20 .....14 A5
ch Av KWD/TDW/WH KT20 .....24 A1
ch Av KWD/TDW/WH KT20 .....24 A1
ch Av KWD/TDW/WH KT20 .....24 B1
ch Av KWD/TDW/WH KT20 .....24 A1

botts Ri REDH RH1 .....35 E2
inger Cl RDKG RH5 .....40 C5
inger Rd REDH RH1 .....45 G2
tion Cl HORL RH6 .....57 C2
orn Gv KWD/TDW/WH KT20 .....14 B4
res Gdns KWD/TDW/WH KT20 .....6 C4
lers La RDKG RH5 .....29 E1
ates La ASHTD KT21 .....3 H3
any Park Rd LHD/OX KT22 .....3 E4
e Albanys REDH RH1 .....33 G1
pertine Cl EW KT17 .....6 B1
pert Rd ASHTD KT21 .....4 B3
HORL RH6 .....57 E3
REDH RH1 .....26 C4
pert Rd North REIG RH2 .....33 F3
pion Ms REIG * RH2 .....45 E1
pion Rd REIG RH2 .....34 A5
bury Keep HORL RH6 .....57 F2
bury Rd REDH RH1 .....26 C4
cocks Cl KWD/TDW/WH KT20 .....7 E5
cocks La KWD/TDW/WH KT20 .....7 F5
ders Rd REIG RH2 .....33 H2
derstead La REDH RH1 .....16 D5
exander Godley Cl ASHTD KT21 .....4 B4
exander Rd REIG RH2 .....44 C2
en Rd GT/LBKH KT23 .....18 D1
ingham Rd REIG RH2 .....44 C2
um Gv KWD/TDW/WH KT20 .....13 F1
ma Rd REIG RH2 .....33 H3
pine Rd REDH RH1 .....35 E1
thorne Rd REDH RH1 .....46 A1
nbleside Cl REDH RH1 .....46 B4
ingel Pl REIG * RH2 .....44 D1
asell Rd DORK RH4 .....29 F5
berdele Rd LHD/OX KT22 .....3 E3
pley Rd REIG RH2 .....44 C2
pple Tree Cl GT/LBKH KT23 .....9 E5
pril Cl ASHTD KT21 .....4 B3
quila Ct ASHTD KT21 .....11 E1
bour Cl LHD/OX KT22 .....9 H3
butus Rd REIG RH2 .....45 E1
butus Rd REDH RH1 .....35 E3
e Arcade REDH * RH1 .....35 E3
rchway Ms DORK RH4 .....29 E5
den Cl DORK RH4 .....44 D3
rdshiel Dr REDH RH1 .....45 G1
rne Gv HORL RH6 .....56 D1
rundel Rd DORK RH4 .....40 A4
sh Cl KWD/TDW/WH KT20 .....31 E1
REDH RH1 .....26 C5
shcombe Rd DORK RH4 .....29 E4
REDH RH1 .....26 C2
shcombe Ter
KWD/TDW/WH KT20 .....6 B5
shdale GT/LBKH KT23 .....19 E1
shdown Cl REIG RH2 .....44 D3
shdown Rd REIG RH2 .....44 D3
sh Dr REDH RH1 .....46 A1
shleigh Cl HORL RH6 .....56 D3
shley Cl GT/LBKH KT23 .....8 B5
shley Cottages ASHTD * KT21 .....4 B4
shley Rd DORK RH4 .....39 E4
EPSOM KT18 .....5 H2

B

Ashtead Woods Rd ASHTD KT21 .....3 G2
Ashurst Dr KWD/TDW/WH KT20 .....21 H5
Ashurst Rd KWD/TDW/WH KT20 .....13 F1
Ashwood Pk KWD/TDW/WH KT22 .....9 E3
Aston Cl ASHTD KT21 .....3 G3
Aston Wy EPSOM KT18 .....5 H1
Atherfield Rd REDH RH1 .....45 E2
Atkinson Ct HORL * RH6 .....57 F4
Atwood GT/LBKH KT23 .....8 A4
Aurum Cl HORL RH6 .....57 F4
Avenue Cl KWD/TDW/WH KT20 .....13 F2
Avenue Gdns HORL RH6 .....57 G4
The Avenue HORL RH6 .....56 D4
KWD/TDW/WH KT20 .....13 F2
RDKG RH5 .....30 C4
REDH RH1 .....47 E2
Avondale Cl HORL RH6 .....56 D1
Axes La REDH RH1 .....54 C1

Babylon La KWD/TDW/WH KT20 .....24 D2
Baden Dr HORL RH6 .....56 C2
Badingham Dr LHD/OX KT22 .....9 C3
Bagot Cl ASHTD KT21 .....4 B1
Bailey Rd DORK RH4 .....39 E2
Bakehouse Rd HORL RH6 .....56 D1
Balchins La DORK RH4 .....38 C2
Balcombe Gdns HORL RH6 .....57 G4
Balcombe Rd HORL RH6 .....57 F2
The Ballands North
LHD/OX KT22 .....9 G2
The Ballands' South
LHD/OX KT22 .....9 G3
Ballantyne Dr
KWD/TDW/WH KT20 .....14 B1
Ballards Gn KWD/TDW/WH KT20 .....7 E4
Balquhain Cl ASHTD KT21 .....3 H2
Bancroft Cl REIG RH2 .....33 H4
Bancroft Rd REIG RH2 .....33 G4
Barclay Cl GT/LBKH KT23 .....8 B1
Barfields REDH RH1 .....36 D3
Barley Mow Ct
BRKHM/BTCW RH3 .....31 E4
Barn Cl KWD/TDW/WH * KT20 .....30 B2
Barnett Cl LHD/OX KT22 .....3 F4
Barnett Wood La ASHTD KT21 .....3 G3
Barn Meadow La GT/LBKH KT23 .....8 B4
The Barnyard
KWD/TDW/WH KT20 .....13 E4
Baron's Hurst EPSOM KT18 .....5 E1
Baron's Wy REIG RH2 .....44 C3
Barrett Rd GT/LBKH KT23 .....9 E5
Barrington Ct DORK RH4 .....40 A2
Barrington Rd DORK * RH4 .....40 A2
Bartholemew Ct DORK * RH4 .....40 A2
Basset Dr REIG RH2 .....33 G3
Battlebridge La REDH RH1 .....26 B5
Batts Hi REDH RH1 .....34 B2
Baxter Av REDH RH1 .....34 C4
Bay Cl HORL RH6 .....53 G5
Bayeux KWD/TDW/WH KT20 .....13 H2
Bayfield Rd HORL RH6 .....56 C2
Bayhorne La HORL RH6 .....57 G5
Baythorn La HORL RH6 .....57 G5
Bay Tree Av LHD/OX KT22 .....3 E5
Beacon Cl BNSTD SM7 .....6 B1
Beaconsfield Rd EPSOM KT18 .....5 F4
Beacon Wy BNSTD SM7 .....6 B1
Beales Rd GT/LBKH KT23 .....18 D1
Bears Den KWD/TDW/WH KT20 .....14 B2
Beattie Cl GT/LBKH KT23 .....8 B4
Beauclare Cl ASHTD KT21 .....10 D1
Beaufort Cl REIG RH2 .....33 F3
Beaufort Rd REIG RH2 .....33 F3
Beaumonts REDH RH1 .....53 H2
Beech Cl DORK RH4 .....28 D5
Beech Crs KWD/TDW/WH KT20 .....22 A5
Beechdene ASHTD KT21 .....4 B4
Beechdene KWD/TDW/WH KT20 .....13 F2
Beech Dr KWD/TDW/WH KT20 .....14 B2
REIG RH2 .....34 B4
Beechen La KWD/TDW/WH KT20 .....14 B5

Beeches Cl KWD/TDW/WH KT20 .....14 C3
The Beeches BNSTD SM7 .....7 H1
LHD/OX KT22 .....9 G4
Beeches Wd
KWD/TDW/WH KT20 .....14 C2
Beech Gv KWD/TDW/WH KT18 .....6 B2
GT/LBKH KT23 .....18 C2
Beech Holt LHD/OX KT22 .....10 C2
Beech Rd REDH RH1 .....26 C1
REIG RH2 .....33 G1
Beechwood
KWD/TDW/WH * KT20 .....30 D1
Beechwood Av
KWD/TDW/WH KT20 .....14 C1
Beechwood Pk LHD/OX KT22 .....10 C2
Beechwood Vls REDH RH1 .....54 A4
Beehive Wy REIG RH2 .....44 D3
The Belfry REDH * RH1 .....34 D3
Bell Crs COUL/CHIP CR5 .....16 B1
Bell La LHD/OX KT22 .....9 F3
Bell Lane Cl LHD/OX KT22 .....9 F3
Bell St REIG RH2 .....33 G4
Bellwether La REDH RH1 .....55 H3
Belmont Rd LHD/OX KT22 .....10 A2
REIG RH2 .....34 A5
Benhams Dr HORL RH6 .....57 E1
Bennetts Farm Pl GT/LBKH KT23 .....8 B5
Bentsbrook Cl RDKG RH5 .....40 B5
Bentsbrook Pk RDKG RH5 .....40 B5
Bentsbrook Rd RDKG RH5 .....40 B5
Beresford Rd DORK RH4 .....40 A1
The Berkeleys LHD/OX KT22 .....9 G4
Berry Meade ASHTD KT21 .....4 B2
Berry Wk ASHTD KT21 .....4 B4
Betchets Green Rd RDKG RH5 .....48 C5
Beverley Hts REIG RH2 .....33 H2
Bickney Wy LHD/OX KT22 .....9 E2
Bidhams Crs
KWD/TDW/WH KT20 .....13 G1
The Bield REIG RH2 .....44 C1
Big Common La REDH RH1 .....36 D3
Birchgate Ms
KWD/TDW/WH * KT20 .....13 G1
Birch Gv KWD/TDW/WH KT20 .....14 A4
Birchway REDH RH1 .....46 B1
Birchwood Cl HORL RH6 .....57 F2
Birchwood La CTHM CR3 .....17 H5
Birkheads Rd REIG RH2 .....33 G3
Blackborough Cl REIG RH2 .....34 A4
Blackborough Rd REIG RH2 .....34 B4
Blackbrook Rd RDKG RH5 .....49 E1
The Blackburn GT/LBKH KT23 .....8 B4
Blackhorse La REIG RH2 .....24 D4
Blacklands Meadow REDH RH1 .....36 A3
Blacksmith Cl ASHTD KT21 .....4 B4
Blackstone Cl REIG RH2 .....34 C5
Blackstone Hl REDH RH1 .....34 C5
Blackthorn Cl REIG RH2 .....45 E1
Blackthorn Rd GT/LBKH KT23 .....19 E1
Blackthorn Rd REIG RH2 .....45 E1
Blades Cl LHD/OX KT22 .....3 A5
Blanford Rd REIG RH2 .....34 B5
Bletchingley Cl REDH RH1 .....26 C4
Bletchingley Rd REDH RH1 .....26 C4
REDH RH1 .....27 E4
Blue Leaves Av COUL/CHIP CR5 .....16 D1
Blundell Av HORL RH6 .....56 D3
Boleyn Wk LHD/OX KT22 .....2 D5
Bolsover Gv REDH RH1 .....27 E4
Bolters Rd HORL RH6 .....57 E1
Bolters Rd South HORL RH6 .....56 D1
Bond's La RDKG RH5 .....48 B2
Bonehurst Rd HORL RH6 .....54 A4
Bonnys Rd REIG RH2 .....32 D4
Bonsor Dr KWD/TDW/WH KT20 .....14 A2
Bookham Ct LHD/OX KT22 .....8 B3
Bookham Gv GT/LBKH KT23 .....18 D1
The Borough RDKG RH5 .....48 B2
Boterys Cross REDH * RH1 .....36 D3
Bourne Gv ASHTD KT21 .....3 H4
Bourne Rd REDH RH1 .....26 C5
Bower Hill Cl REDH RH1 .....47 E2
Bower Hill La REDH RH1 .....35 H5
Bowyers Cl ASHTD KT21 .....4 B3
Boxhill Rd DORK RH4 .....30 A4

Boxhill Wy BRKHM/BTCW RH3 .....41 H3
Box Tree Wk REDH RH1 .....45 E2
Bracken Cl GT/LBKH KT23 .....8 B4
Brackenside HORL RH6 .....57 F2
Bradley La DORK RH4 .....29 F2
Braes Md REDH RH1 .....36 A5
Brakey Hi REDH RH1 .....37 G4
Bramble Cl REDH RH1 .....46 A1
Bramble Hall La
KWD/TDW/WH * KT20 .....30 B2
Brambletye Park Rd REDH RH1 .....45 H1
Bramble Wk REDH * RH1 .....46 A1
Bramblewood REIG RH2 .....26 B4
Bramley Cl REDH RH1 .....45 G1
Bramley Wk HORL RH6 .....57 G3
Bramley Wy ASHTD KT21 .....4 B2
Brandsland REIG RH2 .....44 D3
Breech La KWD/TDW/WH KT20 .....13 E5
Bremner Av HORL RH6 .....56 D2
Brewer St REIG RH2 .....37 E1
Brew House Rd
BRKHM/BTCW RH3 .....41 H3
Briars Wd HORL RH6 .....57 G2
Bridges Cl HORL RH6 .....57 H3
Bridge St LHD/OX KT22 .....10 A2
Brier Lea KWD/TDW/WH KT20 .....24 B1
Brier Rd KWD/TDW/WH KT20 .....6 B4
Brightlands Rd REIG RH2 .....34 A2
Brighton Rd HORL RH6 .....56 D3
KWD/TDW/WH KT20 .....24 B1
REDH RH1 .....34 D4
REDH RH1 .....54 A2
Brighton Ter REDH * RH1 .....34 D5
The Brindles BNSTD SM7 .....7 F2
Broadfield Cl
KWD/TDW/WH KT20 .....6 C5
Broadhurst ASHTD KT21 .....4 A1
Broadhurst Gdns REIG RH2 .....44 D2
Broadlands HORL RH6 .....57 G2
Broadmead ASHTD KT21 .....4 A3
HORL RH6 .....57 G2
REDH * RH1 .....26 C3
Broad Wk COUL/CHIP CR5 .....16 A2
KWD/TDW/WH KT20 .....6 C4
Brockham Hill Pk
KWD/TDW/WH KT20 .....31 E1
Brockhamhurst Rd
BRKHM/BTCW RH3 .....49 H1
Brockham La
BRKHM/BTCW RH3 .....30 C4
Brodrick Gv GT/LBKH KT23 .....18 C1
Brokes Crs REIG RH2 .....33 G2
Brokes Rd REIG RH2 .....33 G2
Brook Cl DORK RH4 .....29 G4
Brookers Cl ASHTD KT21 .....3 G2
Brookfield Cl REDH RH1 .....46 A5
Brooklands Wy REDH RH1 .....34 C2
Brook Rd REDH RH1 .....26 C3
REDH RH1 .....34 D5
Brookside RDKG RH5 .....49 F5
Brook Va RDKG RH5 .....48 B2
Brook Wy LHD/OX KT22 .....3 E3
Brookwood HORL RH6 .....57 F2
Broome Cl EPSOM KT18 .....22 B1
Broomfield Pk DORK RH4 .....39 E2
Broomhurst Ct DORK RH4 .....40 A2
Browning Rd LHD/OX KT22 .....9 F5
Brownlow Rd REDH RH1 .....34 C4
The Brow REDH RH1 .....46 A4
Brympton Cl DORK RH4 .....40 A3
Buckhurst Cl REDH RH1 .....34 C2
Buckingham Rd RDKG RH5 .....48 C4
Buckland Rd
KWD/TDW/WH KT20 .....24 B3
REIG RH2 .....32 D3
Buckles Wy BNSTD SM7 .....7 E5
Budgen Dr REDH RH1 .....35 E1
Buffers La LHD/OX KT22 .....3 E4
Bullfinch Cl HORL RH6 .....56 C2
Bull Hl LHD/OX KT22 .....10 A1
Bunbury Wy EW KT17 .....6 B1
Bunce Common Rd REIG RH2 .....50 B3
Burlington Pl REIG RH2 .....33 G3
Burney Cl GT/LBKH KT23 .....9 E5

Burney Rd *RDKG* RH5 ....29 E1
Burnham Dr *REIG* RH2 ....33 G3
Burnhams Rd *GT/LBKH* KT23 ....8 A4
Burnside *ASHTD* KT21 ....4 B3
The Burrell *DORK* RH4 ....39 E2
Burrows Cl *GT/LBKH* KT23 ....8 B4
Burton Cl *REDH* RH1 ....57 E4
Burwood Cl *REIG* RH2 ....34 B4
Bushbury La *BRKHM/BTCW* RH3 ...41 G4
Bushetts Gv *REIG* RH2 ....26 B4
Bushfield Dr *REDH* RH1 ....46 A4
Bushy Rd *GT/LBKH* KT23 ....8 D2
Bushy Shaw *ASHTD* KT21 ....3 G2
Butter Hl *DORK* RH4 ....40 A1
Byron Pl *LHD/OX* KT22 ....10 D1
Byttom Hl *RDKG* RH5 ....20 C2

C

Caberfeigh Pl *REDH* * RH1 ....34 B4
Caen Wood Rd *ASHTD* KT21 ....3 G3
Cage Yd *REIG* * RH2 ....33 G4
Calvert Crs *DORK* RH4 ....29 F4
Calvert Rd *DORK* RH4 ....29 F4
Cambridge Lodge Pk
  HORL * RH6 ....54 A5
Cambridge Sq *REDH* RH1 ....46 A2
Camilla Cl *GT/LBKH* KT23 ....8 D5
Camilla Dr *RDKG* RH5 ....20 A5
Campion Dr *KWD/TDW/WH* KT20 ....6 B5
Canada Av *REDH* RH1 ....46 A3
Canada Rd *REDH* RH1 ....46 A3
Candy Cft *GT/LBKH* KT23 ....18 D1
Cannon Gv *LHD/OX* KT22 ....9 G1
Cannon Side *LHD/OX* KT22 ....9 G2
Cannon Wy *LHD/OX* KT22 ....9 G1
Canons Cl *REIG* RH2 ....33 F3
Canons La *KWD/TDW/WH* KT20 .....7 E4
Canterbury Ct *DORK* * RH4 ....29 E5
Carlton Ct *HORL* * RH6 ....57 F1
Carlton Gn *REDH* RH1 ....34 C1
Carlton Rd *REDH* RH1 ....34 B2
Carlton Tye *HORL* RH6 ....57 H3
Carrington Cl *REDH* RH1 ....34 D3
Cartersmead Cl *HORL* RH6 ....57 F2
Cartmel Dr *REDH* RH1 ....34 C3
Castle Cl *REDH* RH1 ....37 E3
  REIG RH2 ....44 D3
Castle Dr *HORL* RH6 ....57 G5
  REIG RH2 ....44 C3
Castlefield Rd *REIG* RH2 ....33 G3
Castle Gdns *DORK* RH4 ....30 B4
Castle Sq *REDH* RH1 ....37 E3
Castle St *REDH* RH1 ....36 D3
Cavendish Gdns *REDH* RH1 ....35 E4
Cavendish Rd *REDH* RH1 ....35 E4
Caxton Ri *REDH* RH1 ....35 E3
Cayton Rd *COUL/CHIP* CR5 ....16 C2
Cedar Cl *DORK* RH4 ....40 B1
  REIG RH2 ....45 E1
Cedar Dr *LHD/OX* KT22 ....9 G3
The Cedars *LHD/OX* KT22 ....10 D1
  REIG RH2 ....34 B4
Cedar Wk *KWD/TDW/WH* KT20 ....14 B3
Central Pde *HORL* * RH6 ....57 F1
Chadhurst Cl *RDKG* RH5 ....40 D4
Chaffers Md *ASHTD* KT21 ....4 B1
Chaffinch Wy *HORL* RH6 ....56 C2
Chaldon Cl *REDH* RH1 ....45 G1
Chalk La *ASHTD* KT21 ....4 C4
  EPSOM KT18 ....5 F1
Chalkpit La *DORK* RH4 ....29 E4
Chalk Pit Rd *ASHTD* KT21 ....4 E4
  BNSTD SM7 ....7 G3
Chalkpit Ter *DORK* * RH4 ....29 E4
Challenge Ct *LHD/OX* KT22 ....3 F1
Chanctonbury Cha *REDH* RH1 .....35 F5
Chantrey Cl *ASHTD* KT21 ....3 G4
Chantry Cl *HORL* RH6 ....56 D2
Chapel Ct *DORK* * RH4 ....40 A1
Chapel Gv *KWD/TDW/WH* KT20 ....6 C4
Chapel La *DORK* RH4 ....39 E2
  GT/LBKH KT23 ....19 E3
Chapel Rd *KWD/TDW/WH* KT20 ...13 D5
  REDH RH1 ....34 D4
Chapel Wy *KWD/TDW/WH* KT20 ....6 C4
Charlesfield Rd *HORL* RH6 ....56 D2
Charlwood Cl *GT/LBKH* KT23 ....8 D4
Charman Rd *REDH* RH1 ....34 C4
Charm Cl *REDH* RH1 ....56 C2
Chart Cl *RDKG* RH5 ....40 C3
Chart Downs *RDKG* RH5 ....40 C3
Chartfield Rd *REIG* RH2 ....34 A5
Chart Gdns *RDKG* RH5 ....40 C4
Chart La *DORK* RH4 ....40 B1

REIG RH2 ....33 H4
Chart La South *RDKG* RH5 ....40 D3
Chartway *REIG* RH2 ....33 H4
The Chase *ASHTD* KT21 ....3 C3
  KWD/TDW/WH KT20 ....15 C1
  REIG RH2 ....34 B4
Chatelet Cl *HORL* RH6 ....57 F2
Chave Cft *KWD/TDW/WH* * KT20 ...6 C4
Chavecroft Ter
  KWD/TDW/WH * KT20 ....6 C4
Cheam Cl *KWD/TDW/WH* KT20 ....13 F1
Chequers Cl *HORL* RH6 ....57 E2
  KWD/TDW/WH KT20 ....13 E5
Chequers Dr *HORL* RH6 ....57 E2
Chequers La
  KWD/TDW/WH KT20 ....13 E5
Chequers Pl *DORK* RH4 ....40 B1
Cherkley *REIG* * RH5 ....20 D1
Cherkley Hl *RDKG* RH5 ....20 C1
Cherry Green Cl *REDH* RH1 ....46 B1
Cherry Orch *ASHTD* KT21 ....4 C3
Chester Cl *DORK* RH4 ....29 G4
Chesters *HORL* RH6 ....56 C1
Chesterton Dr *REDH* RH1 ....27 E3
Chestnut Cl *KWD/TDW/WH* KT20 ..14 C3
  REDH RH1 ....46 B1
Chestnut Md *REDH* RH1 ....34 C3
Chestnut Pl *ASHTD* KT21 ....4 A4
Chestnut Rd *HORL* RH6 ....57 E1
Chetwode Dr
  KWD/TDW/WH KT20 ....6 D3
Chetwode Rd
  KWD/TDW/WH KT20 ....6 C4
Cheyne Wk *HORL* RH6 ....56 D5
Chichester Cl *DORK* RH4 ....29 F4
Chichester Rd *DORK* RH4 ....29 F3
Chilberton Dr *REDH* RH1 ....26 C5
Childs Hall Dr *GT/LBKH* KT23 ......8 B5
Childs Hall Rd *GT/LBKH* KT23 .....8 B5
Chilmans Dr *GT/LBKH* KT23 ....8 D5
Chilmead Rd * *REDH* RH1 ....34 D3
Chilmead La *REDH* RH1 ....35 H2
The Chine *DORK* * RH4 ....29 E4
Chipstead Cl *REDH* RH1 ....34 D5
Chipstead La *COUL/CHIP* CR5 .....14 D4
Chipstead Rd *BNSTD* SM7 ....7 F2
Christie Cl *GT/LBKH* KT23 ....8 B5
Chrystie La *GT/LBKH* KT23 ....18 D3
Chuck's La *GT/LBKH* KT23 ....13 F4
Church Cl *KWD/TDW/WH* KT20 ....24 B2
  LHD/OX KT22 ....9 F4
Church Ct *REIG* RH2 ....33 H4
Churchfield Rd *REIG* RH2 ....33 F3
Church Gdns *LHD/OX* * KT22 ....3 F5
Church Gn
  KWD/TDW/WH KT20 ....13 E4
Church Hl *REDH* RH1 ....26 B1
  REDH RH1 ....36 B3
Churchill Cl *LHD/OX* KT22 ....9 G3
Church La *COUL/CHIP* CR5 ....16 A2
  CTHM CR5 ....17 G3
  EPSOM KT18 ....12 A5
  REDH RH1 ....37 F3
Church Lane Av *COUL/CHIP* CR5 ..16 B2
Church Lane Dr *COUL/CHIP* CR5 ..16 B2
Church Rd *ASHTD* KT21 ....3 H3
  GT/LBKH KT23 ....8 B3
  HORL RH6 ....56 D4
  LHD/OX KT22 ....10 B2
  REDH RH1 ....45 G1
  REIG RH2 ....44 C1
Church St *BRKHM/BTCW* RH3 .....31 G5
  DORK RH4 ....40 A1
  LHD/OX KT22 ....10 A1
  REIG RH2 ....33 H4
Church Ter *RDKG* * RH5 ....48 C5
Church View *HORL* RH6 ....56 D4
Church Wk *HORL* RH6 ....56 D4
  LHD/OX KT22 ....10 B2
  REIG RH2 ....33 H4
The Circus *LHD/OX* * KT22 ....3 F5
Clare Crs *LHD/OX* KT22 ....3 E3
Claremont Ct *DORK* RH4 ....40 B2
Claremont Rd *REDH* RH1 ....35 H1
Claremount Cl *EPSOM* KT18 ....6 C2
Claremount Gdns *EPSOM* KT18 ....6 C2
Clarence Cl *HORL* * RH6 ....57 H2
Clarence Rd *REDH* RH1 ....45 F2
Clarence Wk *REDH* RH1 ....45 F2
Clarence Wy *HORL* RH6 ....57 H3
Clarendon Ms *ASHTD* * KT21 ......4 A4
Clarendon Rd *REDH* * RH1 ....34 D3
Clare Wd *LHD/OX* KT22 ....3 E3
Claygate Rd *DORK* RH4 ....40 B3
Clayhall La *REIG* RH2 ....44 A2
Clayhall Cl *REIG* RH2 ....51 E1
Clayhall Rd *REIG* RH2 ....50 D2

Clay La *EPSOM* KT18 ....11 H4
  REDH RH1 ....35 G5
Cleardene *DORK* RH4 ....40 B1
Cleeve Rd *LHD/OX* KT22 ....3 E5
Clements Md *LHD/OX* KT22 ....3 E4
Clerks Cft *REDH* RH1 ....37 F3
Clifton Cl *HORL* RH6 ....57 H3
Clifton's La *REIG* RH2 ....32 D3
Clifton Ter *DORK* * RH4 ....40 B2
Cliftonville *DORK* RH4 ....40 B2
Clinton Rd *LHD/OX* KT22 ....10 B3
The Close *BRKHM/BTCW* RH3 .....41 H3
  HORL RH6 ....57 G5
  REIG RH2 ....33 H5
Cloverfields *HORL* RH6 ....57 F2
Clover Hl *COUL/CHIP* CR5 ....16 B1
Clump Av *KWD/TDW/WH* KT20 ....31 E1
Clyde Cl *REDH* RH1 ....35 E3
Coach House Ms *REDH* * RH1 .....34 D5
Coach Rd *BRKHM/BTCW* RH3 .....41 G1
  RDKG RH5 ....30 A4
Coast Hl *RDKG* RH5 ....38 B3
Coast Hill La *DORK* RH4 ....38 C3
Cock La *LHD/OX* KT22 ....9 E2
Cockshot Hl *REIG* RH2 ....44 D1
Cockshot Rd *REIG* RH2 ....44 D1
Colcokes Rd *BNSTD* SM7 ....7 G1
Coldharbour La *DORK* RH4 ....40 A3
  REDH RH1 ....37 H3
Colebrooke Rd *REDH* RH1 ....34 C2
Colesmead Rd *REDH* RH1 ....34 D1
College Crs *REDH* RH1 ....35 E1
Colley La *REIG* RH2 ....33 E3
Colley Manor Dr *REIG* RH2 ....32 D3
Colley Wy *REIG* RH2 ....33 E1
Collingwood Cl *HORL* RH6 ....57 F2
Colman Cl *EPSOM* KT18 ....6 C2
Colman Wy *REDH* RH1 ....34 C2
Common Rd *REDH* RH1 ....45 H1
Commonside *GT/LBKH* KT23 ....8 C2
Coneyberry *REIG* RH2 ....45 E3
Coneybury *REDH* RH1 ....37 G3
Conifer Cl *REIG* RH2 ....33 G2
Coniston Wy *REDH* RH1 ....34 C3
Consort Wy *HORL* RH6 ....57 E3
Consort Wy East *HORL* RH6 ....57 F4
The Coombe *BRKHM/BTCW* RH3 ..31 F1
Cooper's Hill Rd *REDH* RH1 ......36 B3
Copleigh Dr *KWD/TDW/WH* KT20 ..7 E5
Copley Cl *REDH* RH1 ....34 C2
Copley Wy *KWD/TDW/WH* KT20 ...6 D5
Copperfields *LHD/OX* KT22 ....9 E2
Coppice La *REIG* RH2 ....33 E3
Copse La *HORL* RH6 ....57 G2
Copse Rd *REIG* RH2 ....45 E1
The Copse *GT/LBKH* KT23 ....8 D3
  REDH RH1 ....47 E1
Copsleigh Av *REDH* RH1 ....54 A1
Copsleigh Cl *REDH* RH1 ....46 A5
Copsleigh Wy *REDH* RH1 ....46 A5
Copt Hill La *KWD/TDW/WH* KT20 ..7 E5
Copthorne Ct *LHD/OX* * KT22 .....10 A1
Copthorne Rd *LHD/OX* KT22 ....3 F5
Corfe Cl *ASHTD* KT21 ....3 G3
Cormongers La *REDH* RH1 ....35 H3
Corner Farm Cl
  KWD/TDW/WH KT20 ....13 G2
Cornfield Rd *REIG* RH2 ....34 A5
The Coronet *HORL* RH6 ....57 G5
Cotland Acres *REDH* RH1 ....45 F1
Courtlands Crs *BNSTD* SM7 ....7 G1
Court Lodge Rd *HORL* RH6 ....56 C2
Cowslip La *RDKG* RH5 ....20 A3
Coxdean *KWD/TDW/WH* KT20 ....6 C4
Crab Hill La *REDH* RH1 ....47 F3
Crabtree Cl *GT/LBKH* KT23 ....19 E1
Crabtree Dr *LHD/OX* KT22 ....10 C4
Crabtree La *GT/LBKH* KT23 ....19 E1
  LHD/OX KT22 ....22 A1
  RDKG RH5 ....19 H5
Craddocks Av *ASHTD* KT21 ....4 B1
Cradhurst Cl *DORK* RH4 ....39 E2
Crakell Rd *REIG* RH2 ....34 A5
Crampshaw La *ASHTD* KT21 ....4 B5
Cranbourne Cl *HORL* * RH6 ....57 F1
Cranston Cl *REIG* RH2 ....33 H5
Cray Av *ASHTD* KT21 ....4 A1
Crescent Ct *HORL* * RH6 ....57 E5
Crescent Rd *REDH* RH1 ....37 E3
  REIG RH2 ....44 C1
The Crescent *HORL* RH6 ....57 E5
  LHD/OX KT22 ....10 B2
  REDH * RH1 ....45 F2
  REIG RH2 ....33 H4
Crescent Wy *HORL* RH6 ....57 E5
Cressall Cl *LHD/OX* KT22 ....3 F5
Cressall Md *LHD/OX* KT22 ....3 F5

Crewdson Rd *HORL* RH6 57
Cricket Hl *REDH* RH1 47
Croffets *KWD/TDW/WH* KT20 13
Croft Av *DORK* RH4 29
Crofton *REDH* RH1 4
Cromwell Rd *REDH* RH1 34
Cronks Hl *REIG* RH2 34
Cronks Hill Cl *REDH* RH1 45
Cronks Hill Rd *REIG* RH2 45
Crossland Rd *REDH* RH1 35
Cross Oak La *REDH* RH1 54
Cross Rd *KWD/TDW/WH* KT20 ...13
Crossways La *REIG* RH2 25
The Crossways *REDH* RH1 26
Croydon Rd *REIG* RH2 34
Crutchfield La *HORL* RH6 52
Cuddington Cl
  KWD/TDW/WH KT20 6
Culverhay *ASHTD* KT21 4
Cunliffe Cl *EPSOM* KT18 11
Curtis Rd *DORK* RH4 28

D

Dale Vw *EPSOM* KT18 11
Daneshill Cl *REDH* RH1 34
Daneshill La *REDH* RH1 34
Darcy Pl *ASHTD* KT21 4
Darcy Rd *ASHTD* KT21 4
Darenth Wy *HORL* RH6 56
Dawnay Rd *GT/LBKH* KT23 18
Daymerslea Rdg *LHD/OX* KT22 ...10
Dayseys Hl *REDH* RH1 55
Dean La *REDH* RH1 16
Deanoak La *REIG* RH2 51
Deans Cl *KWD/TDW/WH* KT20 ...13
Deans La *KWD/TDW/WH* KT20 ...13
  REDH RH1 36
Deans Rd *REDH* RH1 26
De Burgh Gdns
  KWD/TDW/WH KT20 6
De Burgh Pk *BNSTD* SM7 7
Deepdene Av *RDKG* RH5 40
  DORK RH4 29
Deepdene Avenue Rd
  DORK RH4 29
Deepdene Dr *RDKG* RH5 29
Deepdene Gdns *DORK* RH4 29
Deepdene Park Rd *RDKG* RH5 29
Deepdene V *DORK* RH4 29
Deepdene Wd *RDKG* RH5 40
Deepfields *HORL* RH6 56
Deerings Rd *REIG* RH2 33
Deerleap Rd *DORK* RH4 38
Delabole Rd *REDH* RH1 27
Delamere Rd *REIG* RH2 44
Delderfield *ASHTD* KT21 3
Dell Cl *LHD/OX* KT22 9
  RDKG RH5 9
The Dell *HORL* RH6 56
  HORL RH6 57
  KWD/TDW/WH KT20 13
  REIG * RH2 57
Delta Dr *HORL* RH6 57
Delves *KWD/TDW/WH* KT20 13
Dene Cl *HORL* RH6 56
Dene Rd *ASHTD* KT21 4
Dene St *DORK* RH4 40
Dene St Gdns *DORK* RH4 40
Denfield *DORK* RH4 40
Dennis Cl *REDH* RH1 34
Denton Cl *REDH* RH1 46
Dents Gv *KWD/TDW/WH* KT20 ...24
Derby Arms Rd *EPSOM* KT18 5
Derby Cl *EPSOM* KT18 6
Derby Stables Rd *EPSOM* KT18 5
Devitt Cl *ASHTD* KT21 4
Devon Crs *REIG* RH2 34
Devon Rd *REDH* RH1 26
Devonshire Av
  KWD/TDW/WH KT20 31
Diceland Rd *BNSTD* SM7 7
Dilston Rd *LHD/OX* KT22 3
Doctors La *CTHM* CR3 17
Dodds Pk *BRKHM/BTCW* RH3 41
Dome Wy *REDH* RH1 34
Doods Park Rd *REIG* RH2 33
Doods Pl *REIG* * RH2 34
Doods Rd *REIG* RH2 34
Doods Wy *REIG* RH2 34
Doran Dr *REIG* RH2 34
Doran Gdns *REIG* * RH2 34
Doric Dr *KWD/TDW/WH* KT20 7
Dorking Rd *GT/LBKH* KT23 18
  KWD/TDW/WH KT20 23
  LHD/OX KT22 10
Douglas Ms *BNSTD* SM7 7

glas Rd REIG RH2 ....33 G3
ers Green Rd REIG RH2 ....44 D3
vlans Cl GT/LBKH KT23 ....18 C2
vlans Rd GT/LBKH KT23 ....18 D2
vne Cl HORL RH6 ....56 C1
vnland Cl EPSOM KT18 ....6 A1
vnland Gdns EPSOM KT18 ....6 A1
vnland Wy EPSOM KT18 ....6 A1
vns Rd KWD/TDW/WH KT20 ....10 B3
vns Rd EPSOM KT18 ....5 E5
DKG RH5 ....20 C3
Downs LHD/OX KT22 ....10 B5
vns Vw DORK RH4 ....29 G4
ND/TDW/WH KT20 ....13 F1
vnsview Gdns DORK RH4 ....40 B2
vns View Rd GT/LBKH KT23 ....19 E2
vns Wy EPSOM KT18 ....5 H1
/LBKH KT23 ....19 E1
ND/TDW/WH KT20 ....13 F1
vnsway Cl
   ND/TDW/WH KT20 ....13 E5
vns Wd EPSOM KT18 ....6 B2
vnswood REDH RH1 ....34 B2
xe Rd HORL RH6 ....56 C3
xton Cl LHD/OX KT22 ....9 F3
Driftway LHD/OX KT22 ....10 C3
Drive BNSTD SM7 ....7 E2
ORL RH6 ....57 F4
ND/TDW/WH * KT20 ....14 C4
ID/OX KT22 ....9 C2
.... 11 E3
d's Cl ASHTD KT21 ....4 B5
field Rd KWD/TDW/WH KT20 ....13 F4
es Ride RDKG RH5 ....40 D4
can Rd KWD/TDW/WH KT20 ....7 E4
croft Cl REIG RH2 ....33 F4
drey Crs REIG RH2 ....33 H4
gates La BRKHM/BTCW RH3 ....32 D4
lin Cl REDH RH1 ....45 G4
ottar Cl REIG RH2 ....45 F1
raven Av REDH RH1 ....54 B2
Fold Dr REIG RH2 ....45 F1
leston Park Dr GT/LBKH KT23 ....9 E5
hurst La HORL RH6 ....52 D4
on Ct DORK * RH4 ....40 A1

E

sbrook Rd REDH RH1 ....45 H1
swood Rd REDH RH1 ....45 H1
tfield Rd REDH RH1 ....35 F5
tnor Pl REIG * RH2 ....44 C1
tnor Rd REIG RH2 ....44 B1
t Rd REIG RH2 ....33 F3
t St GT/LBKH KT23 ....8 D5
t Wk REIG RH2 ....33 H4
twick Dr GT/LBKH KT23 ....8 D4
twick Park Av GT/LBKH KT23 ....8 D4
twick Rd GT/LBKH KT23 ....8 D5
isham La
   ND/TDW/WH KT20 ....12 D1
leshill RDKG RH5 ....40 C5
nside Rd GT/LBKH KT23 ....8 B4
efield Cl REDH RH1 ....46 A4
eley GT/LBKH KT23 ....8 A4
ngham Rd REIG RH2 ....33 H5
mont Park Rd
   WD/TDW/WH KT20 ....13 E5
mont Wy KWD/TDW/WH KT20 ....7 E4
ersley Cl REDH RH1 ....34 D2
ersley Gdns REDH RH1 ....34 D2
er Wy RDKG RH5 ....40 C5
abeth Ct HORL * RH6 ....57 E3
Cl KWD/TDW/WH KT20 ....22 A5
HD/OX KT22 ....10 B2
croft GT/LBKH * KT23 ....8 C4
Dr LHD/OX KT22 ....10 B2
er Cottages LHD/OX * KT22 ....10 A3
er Ms LHD/OX KT22 ....10 A3
field GT/LBKH KT23 ....8 C3
Gdns KWD/TDW/WH KT20 ....6 C4
hurst Dr DORK RH4 ....40 B3
ore Rd COUL/CHIP CR5 ....15 H1
 Rd LHD/OX KT22 ....10 B2
EDH RH1 ....34 C4
shorn EW KT17 ....6 C1
swood GT/LBKH KT23 ....8 B4
 Tree Cl HORL * RH6 ....57 E1
wood Ct ASHTD KT21 ....3 H2
wood Rd REDH RH1 ....26 A5
erton Rd REIG RH2 ....33 H1
ly Davison Dr EPSOM KT18 ....6 B3
yn La LHD/OX KT22 ....10 A2
yn Rd HORL RH6 ....56 C2

REDH RH1 ....46 A1
Empire Vls REDH RH1 ....54 A4
Endsleigh Rd REDH RH1 ....26 C4
Epsom La North
   KWD/TDW/WH KT20 ....6 B4
Epsom La South
   KWD/TDW/WH KT20 ....13 G1
LHD/OX KT22 ....10 D1
Ermyn Cl LHD/OX KT22 ....10 D1
Ermyn Wy LHD/OX KT22 ....10 D1
Eversfield Rd REIG RH2 ....33 H4
Evesham Cl REIG RH2 ....33 F3
Evesham Rd REIG RH2 ....33 F3
Evesham Rd North REIG RH2 ....33 F3
Ewelands HORL RH6 ....57 G2
Ewood La RDKG RH5 ....49 F5
Eyhurst Cl KWD/TDW/WH KT20 ....14 B4
Eyhurst Pk
   KWD/TDW/WH * KT20 ....15 A3
Eyhurst Spur
   KWD/TDW/WH KT20 ....14 B4

F

The Facade REIG * RH2 ....33 G3
Fairacres KWD/TDW/WH KT20 ....13 G1
Fairfax Av REDH RH1 ....34 D3
Fairfield Av HORL RH6 ....57 E5
Fairfield Cl GT/LBKH KT23 ....8 D5
Fairfield Dr DORK RH4 ....29 F4
Fairfield Rd LHD/OX KT22 ....10 B1
Fairford Cl REIG RH2 ....34 A2
Fairhaven Rd REDH RH1 ....26 A5
Fairholme Crs ASHTD KT21 ....3 C2
Fair La COUL/CHIP CR5 ....15 E5
Fairlawn GT/LBKH KT23 ....8 B4
Fairlawn Dr REDH RH1 ....45 G4
Fairlawns HORL RH6 ....57 F4
Fairs Rd LHD/OX KT22 ....3 E4
Fairstone Ct HORL RH6 ....57 F2
The Fairways REDH RH1 ....45 F2
Falcon La LHD/OX KT22 ....2 D1
Falkland Gv DORK RH4 ....40 A2
Falkland Rd DORK RH4 ....40 A2
Fallowfield Wy HORL RH6 ....57 F2
Farm Cl LHD/OX KT22 ....9 F4
Farm La ASHTD KT21 ....4 D3
Felland Wy REDH RH1 ....45 F3
Feltham Rd REDH RH1 ....45 H1
Fengates Rd REDH RH1 ....34 C4
Fenton Cl REDH RH1 ....35 E4
Fenton Rd REDH RH1 ....35 E4
Ferndale Rd BNSTD SM7 ....7 F1
Ferndown HORL RH6 ....57 E1
Fernlea GT/LBKH KT23 ....8 D4
Ferriers Wy
   KWD/TDW/WH KT20 ....6 C4
Fetcham Common La
   LHD/OX KT22 ....8 D1
Fetcham Park Dr LHD/OX KT22 ....9 G3
The Fieldings HORL RH6 ....57 F2
Fieldview HORL RH6 ....57 F2
Fife Wy GT/LBKH KT23 ....8 C5
Fiona Cl GT/LBKH KT23 ....8 C5
Firlands HORL RH6 ....57 F2
Firs Cl DORK RH4 ....40 A3
The Firs GT/LBKH * KT23 ....8 D5
Fir Tree Cl LHD/OX KT22 ....10 C3
Fir Tree Rd EW KT17 ....6 B1
LHD/OX KT22 ....10 C3
Fir Tree Wk REIG RH2 ....34 B4
Flanchford Rd REIG RH2 ....43 G4
Fleetwood Cl
   KWD/TDW/WH KT20 ....6 D5
Flint Cl GT/LBKH KT23 ....19 E1
REDH RH1 ....34 D3
Flint Cottages LHD/OX * KT22 ......10 B1
Flint Hl DORK RH4 ....40 B3
Flint Hill Cl DORK RH4 ....40 B3
Folly La REDH RH1 ....48 B4
Forest Crs ASHTD KT21 ....4 C1
Forest Dr KWD/TDW/WH KT20 ....14 C1
Forest Wy ASHTD KT21 ....4 C2
Forge Bridge La COUL/CHIP CR5 .....16 B2
Fort La REIG RH2 ....24 D5
Fort Rd KWD/TDW/WH KT20 ....30 D1
Fortyfoot Rd LHD/OX KT22 ....10 C1
Fountain Rd REDH RH1 ....45 G1
Fox Covert LHD/OX KT22 ....9 F4
Fox La GT/LBKH KT23 ....8 B4
REIG RH2 ....33 H1
Foxley Cl REDH RH1 ....46 A4
Frenches Rd REDH RH1 ....35 E2
The Frenches REDH RH1 ....35 E2

Frensham Wy EW KT17 ....6 C1
Freshfield Flats
   KWD/TDW/WH * KT20 ....24 B2
Friars Orch LHD/OX KT22 ....9 F1
Friths Dr REIG RH2 ....33 H1
Fulbourne Cl REDH RH1 ....34 C2
Fullers Wood La REDH RH1 ....35 G4
Furlong Rd DORK RH4 ....39 E2
Furze Cl REDH RH1 ....34 D3
Furzefield Crs REIG RH2 ....45 E1
Furzefield Rd REIG RH2 ....45 E1
Furze Gv KWD/TDW/WH KT20 ....14 B1
Furze Hl KWD/TDW/WH KT20 ....14 B1
Furzehill REDH RH1 ....34 C3
Furze Pl REDH * RH1 ....34 D3

G

The Gables BNSTD SM7 ....7 F2
Gadbrook Rd
   BRKHM/BTCW RH3 ....42 B4
Gale Crs BNSTD SM7 ....7 G2
Garden Cl LHD/OX KT22 ....10 C4
Gardener's Wk GT/LBKH KT23 ....18 D1
Garden Wk COUL/CHIP CR5 ....16 B1
Garibaldi Rd REDH RH1 ....34 D5
Garlands Rd LHD/OX KT22 ....10 B1
REDH RH1 ....34 D4
Garlichill Rd EPSOM KT18 ....6 B2
Garrard Rd BNSTD SM7 ....7 G1
Garratts La BNSTD SM7 ....7 F1
The Garstons GT/LBKH KT23 ....8 B5
Gatesden Cl LHD/OX KT22 ....9 G3
Gatesden Rd LHD/OX KT22 ....9 G3
Gatton Bottom REIG RH2 ....25 H3
Gatton Cl REIG RH2 ....34 A1
Gatton Park Rd REDH RH1 ....34 B1
Gatton Rd REIG RH2 ....34 A1
Gaveston Rd LHD/OX KT22 ....3 E5
Gayler Cl REDH RH1 ....37 H4
Gayton Cl ASHTD KT21 ....4 A3
Gaywood Rd ASHTD KT21 ....4 B5
Gerrards Md BNSTD SM7 ....7 F1
Gilmais GT/LBKH KT23 ....9 E5
Gimcrack Hl LHD/OX KT22 ....10 B2
Glade Spur KWD/TDW/WH KT20 ....14 D1
The Glade KWD/TDW/WH KT20 ....14 D1
LHD/OX KT22 ....8 C2
Gladstone Rd ASHTD KT21 ....3 H3
Glebe Cl GT/LBKH KT23 ....18 C1
Glebe Rd ASHTD KT21 ....3 H3
COUL/CHIP CR5 ....16 B4
DORK RH4 ....39 H1
The Glebe HORL RH6 ....56 D3
REIG RH2 ....51 H1
Gledhow Wd
   KWD/TDW/WH KT20 ....14 D2
Glen Cl KWD/TDW/WH KT20 ....14 A3
Glenfield Cl BRKHM/BTCW RH3 ....41 H2
Glenfield Rd BRKHM/BTCW RH3 ....41 H2
Glenheadon Cl LHD/OX KT22 ....10 D3
Glenheadon Ri LHD/OX KT22 ....10 D3
Glenwood RDKG RH5 ....40 C3
Glory Md DORK RH4 ....40 A4
Gloucester Rd REDH RH1 ....34 D3
Glover's Rd REIG RH2 ....33 H5
Godstone Rd REDH RH1 ....37 G3
Goldcrest Cl HORL RH6 ....56 D3
Goldstone Farm Vw
   GT/LBKH * KT23 ....18 C3
Goodwood Rd REDH RH1 ....34 D2
Goodwyns Rd DORK RH4 ....40 B4
Gordon Ct REDH * RH1 ....45 H1
Gordon Rd REDH RH1 ....35 E1
Gorse Cl KWD/TDW/WH KT20 ....6 B5
Gower Rd HORL RH6 ....56 C3
Granary Cl HORL RH6 ....57 F2
Grand Stand Rd EPSOM KT18 ....5 H4
Grange Cl LHD/OX KT22 ....3 F5
REDH RH1 ....37 F3
REIG RH2 ....26 B3
Grange Dr REDH RH1 ....26 B3
Grangemount LHD/OX KT22 ....3 F5
Grange Rd LHD/OX KT22 ....3 F5
Grantwood Cl REDH RH1 ....46 A4
Grassmere HORL RH6 ....57 F2
Gravel Hl LHD/OX KT22 ....10 A1
Gray's La ASHTD KT21 ....4 B4
Grays Wd HORL RH6 ....57 G3
Great Ellshams BNSTD SM7 ....7 G1
Greatlake Ct HORL * RH6 ....57 F2
Great Tattenhams EPSOM KT18 ....6 C3
Greenacres GT/LBKH KT23 ....28 C4
Greenfields Cl HORL RH6 ....56 C1
Greenfields Rd HORL RH6 ....56 C1
Greenhayes Cl REIG RH2 ....34 A4

Green La ASHTD KT21 ....3 G2
KWD/TDW/WH KT20 ....24 B1
LHD/OX KT22 ....10 D1
REDH RH1 ....34 C2
REDH RH1 ....44 A2
REDH RH1 ....55 F2
REIG RH2 ....33 F4
REIG RH2 ....50 C3
Greensand Cl REDH RH1 ....26 D3
Greensand Rd REDH RH1 ....35 E3
Greensand Wy
   BRKHM/BTCW RH3 ....31 E5
   BRKHM/BTCW RH3 ....32 A4
   DORK RH4 ....39 G2
   RDKG RH5 ....28 B4
   REDH RH1 ....36 C4
   REDH RH1 ....45 G2
   REDH RH1 ....47 H1
   REIG RH2 ....33 F4
The Green KWD/TDW/WH KT20 ....13 H3
LHD/OX KT22 ....9 F4
Greenway GT/LBKH KT23 ....8 D3
Green Wy REDH RH1 ....34 C2
Greenways KWD/TDW/WH KT20 ....13 E5
Greenways Dr REDH RH1 ....46 A4
Grendon Cl HORL RH6 ....56 D1
Greville Cl ASHTD KT21 ....4 A4
Greville Ct GT/LBKH KT23 ....8 D5
Greville Park Av ASHTD KT21 ....4 A3
Greville Park Rd ASHTD KT21 ....4 A3
Greystones Cl REIG RH2 ....45 F1
Greystones Dr REIG RH2 ....34 A2
Griffin Ct ASHTD * KT21 ....4 A4
Griffin Wy GT/LBKH KT23 ....18 C1
Grosvenor Ms REIG RH2 ....44 D2
Grosvenor Rd EPSOM KT18 ....5 C4
Grovehill Rd REDH RH1 ....34 C4
Grove Rd ASHTD KT21 ....4 B3
HORL RH6 ....56 C2
Groveside GT/LBKH KT23 ....18 C2
Groveside Cl GT/LBKH KT23 ....18 C2
The Grove CTHM CR3 ....17 H1
HORL RH6 ....57 F4
Guildford Rd DORK RH4 ....38 D3
GT/LBKH KT23 ....18 B2
LHD/OX KT22 ....9 F5
Gurney's Cl REDH RH1 ....34 D5

H

Haigh Crs REDH RH1 ....46 B1
Hale Pit Rd GT/LBKH KT23 ....19 E1
Hales Oak GT/LBKH KT23 ....19 E1
Hambledon Hl EPSOM KT18 ....5 E1
Hambledon Pl GT/LBKH KT23 ....8 E1
Hambledon V REDH RH1 ....5 E1
Hamilton Pl KWD/TDW/WH KT20 ....14 B3
Hampstead La DORK RH4 ....39 H2
Hampstead Rd DORK RH4 ....39 H4
Hampton Rd REDH RH1 ....45 H4
Hanover Cl REDH RH1 ....26 C3
Hanover Ct DORK RH4 ....39 H1
Hanworth Rd REDH RH1 ....45 H4
Harden Farm Cl COUL/CHIP CR5 ......16 C1
Harding Rd EPSOM KT18 ....5 C4
Hardwicke Rd REIG RH2 ....33 G3
Hardwick Rd REDH RH1 ....45 F1
Hardy Cl HORL RH6 ....56 C3
RDKG RH5 ....40 B5
Harecroft DORK RH4 ....40 B3
GT/LBKH KT23 ....8 D3
Harendon KWD/TDW/WH KT20 ....13 G1
Harewood Cl REIG RH2 ....34 A2
Harington Pl REIG RH2 ....33 G2
Harkness Cl EW KT17 ....6 C1
Haroldslea Cl HORL RH6 ....57 G5
Haroldslea Dr HORL RH6 ....57 G5
Harps Oak La REDH RH1 ....15 H5
Harpurs REIG RH2 ....13 H1
Harrington Cl REIG RH2 ....51 E1
Harriotts Cl ASHTD KT21 ....3 H5
Harriotts La ASHTD KT21 ....3 G4
Harrison Cl REIG RH2 ....33 H5
Harrow Cl DORK RH4 ....40 A2
Harrowlands Pk DORK RH4 ....40 B3
Harrow Rd East DORK RH4 ....40 B3
Harrow Rd West DORK RH4 ....40 A3
Harrowsley Ct HORL RH6 ....57 F4
Hart Cl REDH RH1 ....37 H3
Hart Gdns DORK RH4 ....29 F5
Hartington Pl REIG * RH2 ....33 G2
Hart Rd DORK RH4 ....29 F5
Hartspiece Rd REDH RH1 ....46 A1
Hartswood RDKG RH5 ....40 D4
Hartswood Av REIG RH2 ....44 C3
Harvestside HORL RH6 ....57 G3

Harwood Pk REDH RH1 .....54 A3
Hatch Gdns KWD/TDW/WH KT20....6 D5
Hatchgate HORL RH6 .....56 D4
Hatchlands Rd REDH RH1 .....34 C4
Hatch La REDH RH1 .....55 F1
Hatfield Rd ASHTD KT21 .....4 B4
Hathersham La HORL RH6 .....55 F5
Hatherwood ASHTD KT21 .....3 H5
Hawes Rd KWD/TDW/WH KT20 .....6 D5
Hawk's Hl LHD/OX KT22 .....9 H3
Hawks Hill Cl LHD/OX KT22 .....9 H3
Hawks Hill Ct LHD/OX KT22 .....9 H3
Hawkwood Dell GT/LBKH KT23 ...18 C1
Hawkwood Ri GT/LBKH KT23 .....18 C1
Hawthorn Cl REDH RH1 .....46 A4
Hawthorn Wy REDH RH1 .....46 B1
The Hayes EPSOM KT18 .....5 F4
Hayfields HORL RH6 .....57 G2
Hazel Cl REIG RH2 .....45 E1
Hazelhurst HORL RH6 .....57 G2
Hazelmere Cl LHD/OX KT22 .....3 F4
Hazel Pde LHD/OX * KT22 .....9 F4
Hazel Rd REIG RH2.....45 E1
Hazel Wy LHD/OX KT22 .....9 G2
Hazelwood DORK * RH4 .....40 B2
Headley Common Rd
  EPSOM KT18 .....22 B2
Headley Dr KWD/TDW/WH KT20 ....6 B4
Headley Gv KWD/TDW/WH KT20....6 B5
  KWD/TDW/WH KT20 .....22 B3
Headley Heath Ap
  KWD/TDW/WH KT20 .....21 H5
Headley Pde EPSOM * KT18 .....5 F4
Headley Rd ASHTD KT21 .....5 E3
  EPSOM KT18 .....5 E5
  LHD/OX KT22 .....10 C4
  RDKG RH5 .....20 C4
Heathcote
  KWD/TDW/WH KT20 .....13 H1
Heathdene KWD/TDW/WH KT20 ....7 E4
Heath Dr KWD/TDW/WH KT20 .....13 E5
Heather Cl KWD/TDW/WH KT20....14 A2
  REDH RH1 .....35 F1
Heatherlands HORL * RH6 .....57 G2
Heatherside Cl GT/LBKH * KT23 ....8 B5
Heathers Land RDKG RH5.....40 C4
Heathfield Dr REDH RH1 .....45 G4
Heath Hl DORK RH4 .....40 B1
Heathlands REDH RH1.....13 H2
Heath Ri DORK RH4 .....39 E3
Heathside Ct
  KWD/TDW/WH KT20 .....13 F3
Heathside Pl KWD/TDW/WH KT20...6 D3
Hedingham Cl HORL RH6 .....57 G2
Heights Cl BNSTD SM7 .....7 E1
Hemlock Cl KWD/TDW/WH KT20 ...14 A3
Henbit Cl KWD/TDW/WH KT20.....6 B4
Henfold La RDKG RH5 .....49 E4
Heritage Lawn HORL RH6.....57 G2
Heron Ct DORK * RH4 .....29 E5
Herons Wood Ct HORL * RH6.....57 F2
Heston Rd REDH RH1 .....45 H4
Hethersett Cl REIG RH2.....34 A1
Hevers Av HORL RH6 .....56 D2
Hewers Wy KWD/TDW/WH KT20....6 B5
Heymede LHD/OX KT22 .....10 C3
Highacre DORK RH4 .....40 B4
Highcroft Ct GT/LBKH KT23 .....8 C3
Highfields ASHTD KT21 .....4 A4
  LHD/OX KT22 .....9 F4
Highlands Av LHD/OX KT22 .....10 C2
Highlands Cl LHD/OX KT22 .....10 D3
Highlands Pk LHD/OX KT22 .....10 D3
Highlands Rd LHD/OX KT22 .....10 C2
  REDH RH1 .....34 B3
High Meadow Cl DORK RH4.....40 B2
High Rd COUL/CHIP CR5 .....15 G4
High St DORK RH4 .....40 B1
  GT/LBKH KT23 .....8 D5
  HORL RH6.....57 F3
  KWD/TDW/WH KT20 .....13 G5
  LHD/OX KT22 .....10 B2
  REDH RH1 .....26 B3
  REDH RH1 .....34 D3
  REDH RH1 .....36 B4
  REDH RH1 .....37 F3
  REIG RH2 .....33 G4
High Trees Rd REIG RH2.....34 B5
High View Ct REIG * RH2.....34 B4
Highwoods LHD/OX KT22 .....10 C1
Hildenley Cl REDH RH1 .....26 D3
The Hildens DORK RH4 .....39 E3
The Hildens ASHTD KT21 .....4 A4
Hillcrest KWD/TDW/WH * KT20 ...30 D1
Hilley Field La LHD/OX KT22 .....9 E2
Hillfield Cl REDH RH1 .....35 E4
Hillfield Rd REDH RH1 .....35 E4
Hillford Pl REDH RH1.....46 A5

Hill House Dr REIG RH2 .....44 D1
Hill La KWD/TDW/WH KT20 .....14 A1
Hill Pk LHD/OX * KT22 .....3 E4
Hill Park Ct LHD/OX * KT22 .....2 D1
Hill Ri DORK RH4.....29 E4
Hill Rd GT/LBKH KT23.....8 D2
Hillside BNSTD SM7 .....7 E1
  RDKG RH5 .....30 C5
Hillside Gdns
  BRKHM/BTCW RH3 .....30 C4
Hillside Rd ASHTD KT21 .....4 B2
Hilltop Cl LHD/OX KT22 .....10 C3
Hilltop La CTHM CR3 .....27 C5
Hilltop Ri GT/LBKH KT23 .....19 E1
Hilltop Rd REIG RH2.....44 D1
Hill View Cl KWD/TDW/WH KT20...13 C1
Hillview Dr REDH RH1 .....35 E5
Hine Cl COUL/CHIP CR5 .....16 C2
Hitchings Wy REIG RH2 .....44 C3
Hitherwood Cl REDH RH1.....34 B2
Hogscross La COUL/CHIP CR5 .....15 H2
Hogtrough La REDH RH1 .....35 H5
Holcon Ct REDH RH1 .....35 E1
Hole Hl DORK RH4 .....38 D1
Holland Cl REDH RH1 .....34 D4
Hollis Rw REDH * RH1 .....45 H1
Holly Hill Dr BNSTD SM7 .....7 G2
Holly Hough
  KWD/TDW/WH KT20 .....21 H5
Holly La East BNSTD SM7 .....7 H1
Holly La West BNSTD SM7 .....7 H2
Holly Rd REIG RH2.....44 D1
Holmbury Rd RDKG RH5.....40 C4
Holmcroft KWD/TDW/WH KT20....13 F5
Holmesdale Pk REDH * RH1 .....36 B4
Holmesdale Rd RDKG RH5 .....40 B5
  REDH RH1 .....47 F1
  REIG RH2 .....33 H3
Holmesdale Ter RDKG * RH5 .....40 B5
Holmethorpe Av REDH RH1.....35 F1
Holmwood View Rd RDKG RH5....48 B2
Holsart Cl KWD/TDW/WH KT20 ...13 F2
Home Cl LHD/OX KT22.....9 F1
Home Farm Cl
  BRKHM/BTCW RH3 .....31 G5
  EPSOM KT18 .....6 D2
Homefield Cl HORL RH6 .....57 F2
  LHD/OX KT22 .....10 C1
Homefield Gdns
  KWD/TDW/WH KT20 .....6 C5
Homelands LHD/OX KT22 .....10 C1
Home Meadow BNSTD SM7 .....7 G1
Honeycrock La REDH RH1 .....54 A1
Honeysuckle Cl HORL RH6 .....57 G2
Hooley La REDH RH1 .....34 D5
The Hoppety KWD/TDW/WH KT20 13 H2
Horley Lodge La REDH RH1.....53 H3
Horley Rd REDH RH1 .....45 H4
Horley Rw HORL RH6 .....56 D2
Hornbeam Rd REIG RH2.....45 E2
Horsecroft BNSTD * SM7 .....7 F2
Horsecroft Mdw BNSTD * SM7 .....7 G1
Horsham Rd DORK RH4 .....40 A2
Howard Cl ASHTD KT21.....4 B3
  KWD/TDW/WH KT20 .....12 D5
  LHD/OX KT22 .....10 C3
Howard Pl REIG RH2 .....33 G2
Howard Rd DORK RH4 .....40 A1
  GT/LBKH KT23 .....18 D2
  RDKG * RH5 .....40 C5
  REIG RH2 .....33 H5
Huddleston Crs REDH RH1 .....26 D3
Hudsons KWD/TDW/WH KT20.....13 H1
Hulton Cl LHD/OX KT22 .....10 C3
Humphrey Cl LHD/OX KT22 .....9 E1
Huntersfield Cl REIG RH2 .....34 A1
Huntingdon Rd REDH * RH1 .....34 D4
Hurst Cl EPSOM KT18.....12 A4
Hurst Dr KWD/TDW/WH KT20 .....23 E1
Hurst La EPSOM KT18 .....12 B2
Hurstleigh Cl REDH RH1 .....34 D1
Hurstleigh Dr REDH RH1.....34 D2
Hurst Rd EPSOM KT18.....12 B3
  HORL RH6.....56 C2
Hutchins Wy HORL RH6 .....56 D1

Ifield Cl REDH RH1.....45 G2
Ifold Rd REDH RH1.....46 A1
Imperial Pk LHD/OX * KT22 .....3 E5
Inholms La RDKG RH5.....40 C5
Institute Rd DORK RH4.....39 E2
Ironsbottom REIG RH2.....52 B4
Isbells Dr REIG RH2 .....44 D1
Ivydene REDH RH1.....46 B4

Jasmine Cl REDH RH1 .....46 A4
Jason Cl REDH RH1 .....45 G4
Jennings Wy HORL RH6 .....57 H5
Jennys Wy COUL/CHIP CR5 .....16 C2
Jolliffe Rd REDH RH1 .....26 C1
Jordans Cl REDH RH1 .....46 A4
Josephine Av
  KWD/TDW/WH KT20 .....24 B2
Josephine Cl
  KWD/TDW/WH KT20 .....24 B2
Jubilee Ter BRKHM/BTCW RH3 .....42 A3
  DORK RH4 .....29 F5
Junction Rd DORK RH4 .....40 A1
June La REDH RH1 .....54 B1
Juniper Cl REIG RH2.....45 E1
Juniper Rd REIG RH2.....45 E1

Keats Av REDH RH1 .....35 E2
Kelsey Cl HORL RH6.....56 D3
Kelvin Av LHD/OX KT22 .....10 A2
Kendal Cl REDH RH1 .....34 B3
Kenilworth Cl BNSTD SM7 .....7 H1
Kennel Cl GT/LBKH KT23 .....9 E4
Kennel La HORL RH6 .....56 B4
  REDH RH1 .....9 E3
Kenrick Sq REDH RH1 .....37 F3
Kentwyns Ri REDH RH1 .....35 E3
Kenya Ct HORL * RH6 .....56 D5
Keppel Rd DORK RH4 .....29 F4
Keswick Av GT/LBKH KT23 .....9 E5
Kidborough Down
  GT/LBKH KT23 .....18 C2
Kidworth Cl REDH RH1 .....56 D1
Kilmarnock Pk REIG RH2 .....33 H3
Kiln La BRKHM/BTCW RH3 .....30 D5
  HORL RH6.....56 C3
Kimberley Ri HORL RH6 .....56 C3
Kingfisher Ct DORK * RH4 .....29 E4
Kingfisher Dr REDH RH1 .....35 E1
Kings Av REDH RH1 .....45 G1
  REDH RH1 .....9 E3
Kingsbrook LHD/OX KT22.....3 E3
Kings Ct KWD/TDW/WH KT20 .....13 G2
Kingscroft Rd LHD/OX KT22.....3 F5
Kings Cross La REDH RH1.....47 F2
Kingsdene KWD/TDW/WH KT20 ...13 F1
Kingslea LHD/OX KT22 .....3 E5
Kingsley Cl HORL RH6 .....56 D1
Kingsley Gv REIG RH2 .....44 C2
Kingsley Rd HORL RH6 .....56 D1
Kings Md REDH RH1 .....47 E1
Kings Mill La REDH RH1 .....46 D3
Kingston Av LHD/OX KT22 .....10 B1
Kingston House Gdns
  LHD/OX * KT22.....10 B1
Kingston Rd LHD/OX KT22.....3 E3
  LHD/OX KT22 .....10 A1
Kingswood Rd
  KWD/TDW/WH KT20 .....13 F1
Kinnersley Mnr REIG * RH2.....53 E2
Kinnersley Wk REIG RH2.....44 C4
Kipings KWD/TDW/WH KT20.....13 H2
Knighton Rd REDH RH1 .....46 A1
Knights Pl REDH RH1 .....35 E3
Knightwood Cl REIG RH2 .....44 C4
Knoll Rd DORK RH4 .....40 A3
The Knolls EW KT17.....6 C1
The Knoll LHD/OX KT22 .....10 C1
The Knowle
  KWD/TDW/WH * KT20 .....13 F1

Ladbroke Gv REDH RH1 .....35 E3
Ladbroke Rd HORL RH6 .....57 E1
  REDH RH1 .....35 E2
Ladyegate Cl RDKG RH5 .....29 H5
Ladyegate Rd RDKG RH5 .....40 C1
Laglands Cl REIG RH2 .....34 A2
Lake La REDH RH1 .....57 G1
Lakeside REDH RH1 .....35 E2
Lake Vw RDKG RH5 .....40 C4
Lambyn Cft HORL RH6 .....57 G2
Landen Pk HORL RH6 .....56 C1
Landscape La LHD/OX KT22 .....8 D3
Lang Cl GT/LBKH KT23.....8 D3
Langley Cl EPSOM KT18.....5 F4
Langley Vale Rd EPSOM KT18.....5 F3

Langshott HORL RH6.....57
Langshott La HORL RH6 57
Langwood Cl REDH RH1.....4
Larch Cl KWD/TDW/WH KT20 15
  REIG RH2 45
Larchwood Cl BNSTD SM7 7
Larksfield HORL RH6 57
Larkspur Wy RDKG RH5 40
The Laurels BNSTD SM7 7
Lavender Cl REDH RH1 46
Lavender Cottages
  LHD/OX * KT22.....10
Lawrence La BRKHM/BTCW RH3...32
Laxton Gdns REDH RH1 26
Leach Gv LHD/OX KT22 10
Leaside GT/LBKH KT23.....9
Leatherhead By-Pass Rd
  LHD/OX KT22.....3
Leatherhead Rd ASHTD KT21.....3
  GT/LBKH KT23 19
Leazes Av CTHM CR3.....17
Lechford Rd HORL RH6.....56
Ledbury Rd REIG RH2 33
Lee Acre DORK * RH4 40
Lee La LHD/OX KT22 22
Leech La LHD/OX KT22 22
Lee St HORL RH6.....56
Leigh Place Rd REIG RH2 43
Leigh Rd BRKHM/BTCW RH3 42
  DORK RH4 39
Leith Vw RDKG RH5 40
Le May Cl HORL RH6.....57
Leret Wy LHD/OX KT22 10
Lesbourne Rd REIG RH2 33
Leslie Rd DORK RH4 29
Levett Rd LHD/OX KT22 3
Lilley Dr KWD/TDW/WH KT20 14
Lime Cl REIG RH2 44
Limes Av HORL RH6 57
The Limes LHD/OX KT22 10
Lime Tree Cl GT/LBKH KT23.....8
Limeway Ter DORK RH4 29
Lince La DORK RH4 39
Lincoln Rd DORK RH4 29
Linden Cl KWD/TDW/WH KT20 6
Linden Ct LHD/OX KT22 10
Linden Gdns LHD/OX KT22 10
Linden Lea DORK * RH4 40
Linden Pit Pth LHD/OX KT22 10
Linden Rd LHD/OX KT22 10
Lindens Cl EHSLY KT24.....
Linkfield Gdns REDH RH1 34
Linkfield La REDH RH1 34
Linkfield St REDH RH1.....34
Links Brow LHD/OX KT22 10
Links Cl ASHTD KT21.....3
Links Pl ASHTD KT21 3
Links Rd ASHTD KT21.....3
Links View Av RDKG RH5 30
Links Wy EHSLY KT24.....18
Linnell Rd REDH RH1 35
Little Bookham St GT/LBKH KT23 ..18
Little Borough
  BRKHM/BTCW RH3 30
Little Chesters
  KWD/TDW/WH * KT20 13
Little Collins REDH * RH1 55
Little Common La REDH RH1.....36
Little Gv DORK * RH4 40
Littleton La REIG RH2 44
Lodgebottom Rd RDKG RH5 21
Lodge Cl LHD/OX KT22.....9
  RDKG RH5 40
Lodge La RDKG RH5.....49
  REDH RH1 53
Lodge Rd LHD/OX KT22.....9
London Rd DORK RH4 29
  REDH RH1 35
  REIG RH2 33
London Rd North
  COUL/CHIP CR5.....16
  REDH RH1 26
London Rd South REDH RH1 26
Lonesome La REIG RH2.....45
  REIG RH2 53
Longbridge Rd HORL RH6 56
Longbridge Wk HORL RH6.....57
Longchamp Cl HORL RH6 57
Long Copse Cl GT/LBKH KT23.....9
Longfield Crs
  KWD/TDW/WH KT20.....6
Longfield Rd DORK RH4 39
Longheath Dr GT/LBKH KT23.....8
Longmeadow GT/LBKH KT23 9
Longmere Gdns
  KWD/TDW/WH KT20.....6
Long Shaw LHD/OX KT22.....3
Long Wk KWD/TDW/WH KT20 6
Lonsdale Rd DORK RH4.....29
Loop Rd EPSOM KT18.....5

ine Gdns *ASHTD* KT21 ....4 A2
dsgrove Cl
  D/TDW/WH KT20 ....6 B5
an Dr *REIG* RH2 ....34 A3
Lorne *GT/LBKH* KT23 ....18 C1
hian Wd *KWD/TDW/WH* KT20...13 F2
elands La
  D/TDW/WH KT20 ....24 D2
e La *KWD/TDW/WH* KT20 ......23 E1
burys *DORK* RH4...............40 A4
er Bridge Rd *REDH* RH1 ....34 D4
er Rd *GT/LBKH* KT23.............18 B1
HD/OX KT22........................9 F3
EIG RH2 ....45 F1
er Shott *GT/LBKH* KT23.........18 D1
eds Cl *DORK* RH4.................40 C4
Lye *KWD/TDW/WH* KT20.......13 G2
den Gdns *REIG* RH2.............44 D1
e Regis Rd *BNSTD* SM7...........7 F2
dale Rd *REDH* RH1 ....34 D1
hurst Rd *REIG* RH2..............44 C2
n Wk *REIG* RH2.....................44 B5
wood Rd *REDH* RH1.............35 E2
ns Ct *DORK* RH4..................40 B1
sdene *KWD/TDW/WH* KT20...24 D2
ood Cl *KWD/TDW/WH* KT20...13 G2

M

botts *KWD/TDW/WH* KT20...13 H1
dox *GT/LBKH* KT23.................8 A4
dox Pk *GT/LBKH* KT23.............8 A3
eira Wk *REIG* RH2.................34 B3
gazine Pl *LHD/OX* KT22..........10 B2
gazine Rd *CTHM* CR3.............17 H2
gnolia Ct *HORL* * RH6...........57 E3
gnolia Wy *RDKG* RH5.............40 D4
zecroft *HORL* RH6.................57 G2
lcolm Gdns *HORL* RH6...........56 B5
ard Cl *HORL* RH6.................57 E1
EIG RH2 ....35 E1
ard Ct *DORK* * RH4..............29 E4
low Cl *WD/TDW/WH* KT20.......6 B4
mstone Av *REDH* RH1...........26 C5
nnamead *EPSOM* KT18............5 G4
namead Cl *EPSOM* KT18..........5 G4
or Cl *HORL* RH6...................56 D3
or Dr *HORL* RH6..................56 D3
orhouse La *GT/LBKH* KT23 ...18 A1
or La *KWD/TDW/WH* KT20......24 C4
or Pl *GT/LBKH* KT23.............18 C1
or Rd *REDH* RH1..................26 C4
EIG RH2 ....33 F2
or Wy *LHD/OX* KT22...............2 A1
sfield Dr *REDH* RH1.............26 D3
lehurst *LHD/OX* KT22.............9 F3
ole Rd *ASHTD* KT21...............3 H1
EDH RH1 ....45 H3
ole Wy *COUL/CHIP* CR5..........16 B1
bles Wy *KWD/TDW/WH* KT20 ...6 D4
gery Cl *KWD/TDW/WH* KT20...24 A4
gery La *KWD/TDW/WH* KT20...24 B4
kedge La *COUL/CHIP* CR5.......15 C1
EIG RH2 ....25 H2
ket Field Rd *REDH* RH1.........34 D3
ketfield Wy *REDH* RH1.........34 D4
k Oak La *LHD/OX* KT22...........8 C1
k St *REIG* RH2......................33 H3
lborough Rd *DORK* RH4.........40 B1
Marld *ASHTD* KT21.................4 B3
ley Rd *DORK* RH4.................40 A4
tineau Dr *DORK* RH4............40 B3
son's Bridge Rd *REDH* RH1...46 B4
sons Paddock *DORK* RH4.....29 E4
ssetts Rd *REDH* RH1............56 D4
thew's St *REIG* RH2.............44 C3
ybury Rd *KWD/TDW/WH* KT20...7 E4
yell Cl *LHD/OX* KT22.............10 C3
yfield *LHD/OX* KT22.............10 C1
yfield Cl *REDH* RH1.............46 A5
yfield Gn *GT/LBKH* KT23........18 C2
ad Av *REDH* RH1..................54 A2
ad Cl *REDH* RH1..................35 E4
ars Ct *GT/LBKH* KT23.............8 C5
ad End *ASHTD* KT21...............4 B2
adowbrook Rd *DORK* RH4.....29 E5
adow La *LHD/OX* KT22............9 E2
adow Rd *ASHTD* KT21.............4 B2
adowside *GT/LBKH* KT23.......8 C3
EIG RH2 ....57 F2
adow Wk
  WD/TDW/WH KT20............13 F4
adow Wy *GT/LBKH* KT23........8 D3
WD/TDW/WH KT20..................7 E2
RH2 ....44 D3

The Mead *ASHTD* KT21.............4 A4
  DORK * RH4....................40 C4
Meadway *EHSLY* KT24.............18 A3
The Meadway *HORL* RH6.........57 G3
Meare Cl *KWD/TDW/WH* KT20...13 G3
Meath Green Av *HORL* RH6.....56 D1
Meath Green La *REDH* RH1.....53 G3
Mede Fld *LHD/OX* KT22............9 F4
Melton Rd *REDH* RH1.............26 C5
Melvinshaw *LHD/OX* KT22......10 C1
Meon Cl *KWD/TDW/WH* KT20....13 F2
Merefield Gdns
  KWD/TDW/WH KT20.............6 D4
Mere Rd *KWD/TDW/WH* KT20...13 F4
Meridian Gv *HORL* RH6...........57 G2
Merland Cl *KWD/TDW/WH* KT20...6 C5
Merland Gn *KWD/TDW/WH* KT20...6 C5
Merland Ri *KWD/TDW/WH* KT20...6 C5
Merrylands Farm *GT/LBKH* KT23...8 B4
Merrylands Rd *GT/LBKH* KT23...8 B3
Merrywood Gv
  KWD/TDW/WH KT20............23 H5
Merrywood Pk *REIG* RH2.......33 H2
Merstham Rd *REDH* RH1.........27 G5
Merton Gdns
  KWD/TDW/WH KT20.............6 D5
Merton Wy *LHD/OX* KT22..........3 E4
The Mews *REIG* * RH2............33 H3
Michael Crs *HORL* RH6...........57 E5
Michelham Gdns
  KWD/TDW/WH KT20.............6 C5
Mickleham Dr *LHD/OX* KT22...20 C1
Middlefield *HORL* RH6...........57 G2
Middlemead Cl *GT/LBKH* KT23...8 C5
Middlemead Rd *GT/LBKH* KT23 ...8 B5
Middle Rd *LHD/OX* KT22..........10 A1
Middle St *BRKHM/BTCW* RH3...30 C5
Mid Holmwood La *RDKG* RH5...48 B2
Mid St *REDH* RH1..................36 B4
  REDH RH1 ....47 F1
Miena Wy *ASHTD* KT21.............3 H2
Millbottom La *RDKG* RH5.......48 D4
Mill Cl *GT/LBKH* KT23.............8 C4
  HORL RH6........................56 C2
Millers Copse *EPSOM* KT18......5 F4
  REDH RH1 ....55 H4
Miller's La *REDH* RH1............55 H4
Millfield La *KWD/TDW/WH* KT20...14 C4
Mill HI *BRKHM/BTCW* RH3.......30 D5
Mill Hill La *BRKHM/BTCW* RH3...30 D5
Mill La *DORK* RH4.................29 F5
  HORL RH6........................56 C2
  LHD/OX KT22....................10 A2
  DORK RH4........................29 F5
  RDKG RH5........................48 C4
Mill Rd *KWD/TDW/WH* KT20.....13 H3
  RDKG RH5........................48 C4
Millside Ct *GT/LBKH* * KT23.....8 C5
Millstead Cl *KWD/TDW/WH* KT20...13 F3
Mill St *REDH* RH1.................34 C5
Millview Cl *REDH* RH1...........34 B2
Mill Wy *LHD/OX* KT22.............10 A2
Millway *REIG* RH2.................34 B4
Milton Av *DORK* RH4.............39 G1
Miltoncourt La *DORK* RH4......39 G1
Milton St *DORK* RH4.............39 G1
Milton Wy *GT/LBKH* KT23........9 E5
Minchin Cl *LHD/OX* KT22........10 A2
Mint Gdns *DORK* RH4.............29 E5
Mint Wk *KWD/TDW/WH* KT20...24 C4
Moat Ct *ASHTD* KT21...............4 A2
Moats La *REDH* RH1...............47 E5
Mogador Rd
  KWD/TDW/WH KT20............24 A3
Mole Cl *KWD/TDW/WH* KT20......9 F1
Mole Valley Pl *ASHTD* KT21......3 H4
Monks Gn *LHD/OX* KT22...........9 F1
Monks Rd *BNSTD* SM7.............7 G2
Monk's Wk *REIG* RH2.............33 H4
Monkswell La *COUL/CHIP* CR5...14 D4
Monson Rd *REDH* RH1...........34 B4
Montfort Ri *REDH* RH1...........53 H2
Montrouge Crs *EW* KT17..........6 C1
Moore's La *DORK* RH4............29 F5
Moorfield *RDKG* * RH5...........48 D4
The Moorings *GT/LBKH* KT23.....8 C5
Moor Pk *HORL* * RH6.............57 F4
Morden Cl *KWD/TDW/WH* KT20...6 D5
Morris Rd *REDH* RH1.............47 E1
Morston Cl *KWD/TDW/WH* KT20...6 C5
Morton *KWD/TDW/WH* KT20...13 H1
Mosford Cl *HORL* RH6............56 C1
Mostyn Ter *REDH* RH1...........35 E5
Motts Hill La
  KWD/TDW/WH KT20............13 E3
Mount Cl *LHD/OX* KT22............9 F4
The Mount Dr *REIG* RH2.........34 A2
Mount Pleasant *EHSLY* KT24...18 A3
Mount Ri *REDH* RH1..............45 F1

Mount St *DORK* RH4..............40 A1
The Mount *KWD/TDW/WH* KT20 ..24 B1
  LHD/OX KT22......................9 G3
Mountview Cl *REDH* RH1.........45 G1
Mountview Dr *REDH* RH1.........45 G1
Mowbray Gdns *DORK* RH4.......29 F4
Murrells Wk *GT/LBKH* KT23......8 C5
The Murreys *ASHTD* KT21.........3 H3
Myrtle Cottages *DORK* * RH4...40 B4
Myrtle Rd *DORK* RH4.............29 E5

N

Nailsworth Crs *REDH* RH1.......26 C5
Nash Gdns *REDH* RH1............34 D2
Netherleigh Pk *REDH* RH1.......47 E2
Netherne La *COUL/CHIP* CR5...16 C2
New Battlebridge La *REDH* RH1...26 B5
New Cswy *REIG* RH2..............44 D2
New Cottages *DORK* * RH4.......39 H2
  REIG * RH2........................32 D2
Newenham Rd *GT/LBKH* KT23...18 C1
New House La *REDH* RH1.........54 D2
Newlands Cl *HORL* RH6...........56 D1
New North Rd *REDH* RH1........44 B2
New Pde *DORK* * RH4.............29 F5
  GT/LBKH * KT23................19 E1
New Rd *KWD/TDW/WH* KT20...13 G3
Newstead Hall *HORL* * 57 H4
Newton Wood Rd *ASHTD* KT21...4 B1
Nightingale Wy *REDH* RH1.......37 G4
Noke Dr *REDH* RH1...............35 E3
Norbury Rd *REIG* RH2............33 F4
Norbury Wy *GT/LBKH* KT23......9 E5
Norfolk Cl *HORL* RH6.............57 E4
Norfolk La *RDKG* RH5............48 B2
Norfolk Rd *DORK* RH4............40 A1
  RDKG RH5........................48 C5
Nork Ri *BNSTD* SM7................6 D1
Norman Cl *KWD/TDW/WH* KT20...6 B5
North Acre *BNSTD* SM7............7 F1
North Cl *RDKG* RH5..............40 C5
North Downs Wy
  BRKHM/BTCW RH3..............22 C5
  DORK RH4........................29 G2
  REDH RH1 ....27 E1
Northfields *ASHTD* KT21.........4 A4
North Md *REDH* RH1.............34 D1
North Rd *REIG* RH2...............44 B2
North Station Ap *REDH* * RH1...47 F1
North St *DORK* RH4...............40 A1
  LHD/OX KT22....................10 A2
  REDH RH1 ....34 D3
North View Crs *EPSOM* KT18......6 C2
Norwood Cl *EHSLY* KT24.........18 A3
Norwood Rd *EHSLY* KT24.........18 A3
Nower Rd *DORK* RH4.............40 A1
Nursery Cl *KWD/TDW/WH* KT20...13 F5
Nursery La *HORL* RH6............56 B4
Nursery Rd *KWD/TDW/WH* KT20...13 F5
Nutcombe La *DORK* RH4.........28 D5
Nutcroft Gv *LHD/OX* KT22........9 G2
Nutfield Marsh Rd *REDH* RH1...35 H1
Nutfield Rd *REDH* RH1...........26 C5
  REDH RH1 ....35 F4
Nuthatch Gdns *REIG* RH2.......45 G3
Nutley La *REIG* RH2...............33 F3
Nutwood Av *BRKHM/BTCW* RH3...31 E5
Nutwood Cl *BRKHM/BTCW* RH3...31 E5
Nyefield Pk *KWD/TDW/WH* KT20...23 G2

O

Oakbank *LHD/OX* KT22............9 E3
Oak Cl *KWD/TDW/WH* KT20.....21 H5
Oakdene *KWD/TDW/WH* KT20....7 E3
Oakdene Cl *BRKHM/BTCW* RH3...42 A1
  GT/LBKH KT23..................19 E2
Oakdene Rd *BRKHM/BTCW* RH3...41 H1
  GT/LBKH KT23....................8 A4
  REDH RH1 ....34 D4
Oak Dr *KWD/TDW/WH* KT20.....21 H5
Oaken Coppice *ASHTD* KT21......4 C4
Oakfield Dr *REIG* RH2............33 G2
Oakfield Rd *ASHTD* KT21..........4 A3
Oak HI *EPSOM* KT18................5 F1
Oakhill Cl *ASHTD* KT21.............3 G3
Oakhill Rd *ASHTD* KT21.............3 G3
  REIG RH2 ....33 H5
Oaklands *HORL* RH6..............57 G3
  LHD/OX KT22......................9 F4
Oaklands Dr *REDH* RH1...........46 B3
Oaklands Wy
  KWD/TDW/WH KT20............13 G2

Oaklawn Rd *LHD/OX* KT22........2 C3
Oak Lodge Dr *REDH* RH1.........54 A2
Oak Rdg *DORK* RH4...............40 B4
Oak Rd *LHD/OX* KT22..............3 E4
  REIG RH2 ....33 H3
Oaks Cl *LHD/OX* KT22.............10 A1
Oakside Ct *HORL* RH6............57 G2
Oakside La *HORL* RH6............57 G2
Oaks La *RDKG* RH5................48 B2
Oaks Rd *REIG* RH2................33 H4
The Oaks *DORK* * RH4............40 B4
Oaks Wy *EPSOM* KT18.............6 B4
Oak Wy *ASHTD* KT21...............4 C1
  REIG RH2 ....34 B5
Oakwood Cl *REDH* RH1...........35 E4
  REDH * RH1......................47 F1
Oakwood Rd *HORL* RH6.........57 E2
  REIG RH2 ....27 G4
Oatfield Rd *KWD/TDW/WH* KT20...13 F1
Oatlands *HORL* RH6..............57 F2
Oatlands Rd
  KWD/TDW/WH KT20.............7 E4
Old Barn Rd *EPSOM* KT18.........5 E2
Old Ct *ASHTD* KT21.................4 A4
Oldfield Gdns *ASHTD* KT21.......3 H4
Oldfield Rd *HORL* RH6...........56 D5
Old Fox Cl *CTHM* CR3.............17 H1
Old Kiln La *BRKHM/BTCW* RH3...31 E4
Old London Rd *EPSOM* KT18......6 A3
  RDKG RH5........................20 C3
Old Mill La *REDH* RH1...........26 B3
Old Pottery Cl *REIG* RH2........44 D1
Old Rectory Cl
  KWD/TDW/WH KT20............13 E4
Old Redstone Dr *REDH* RH1...35 E5
Old Reigate Rd
  BRKHM/BTCW RH3..............31 E4
  DORK RH4........................30 A4
Old Rd *BRKHM/BTCW* RH3.......31 H3
Old School La
  BRKHM/BTCW RH3..............41 G2
Old Station Ap *LHD/OX* KT22...10 A1
Orchard Cl *ASHTD* KT21...........3 H5
  HORL RH6........................56 D2
  LHD/OX KT22......................9 F2
Orchard End *GT/LBKH* KT23......9 E4
Orchard Gdns *EHSLY* KT24.......18 A3
Orchardleigh *LHD/OX* KT22......10 B2
Orchard Rd *DORK* RH4............40 B2
  REIG RH2 ....32 D2
The Orchard *HORL* * RH6.......57 E3
  RDKG RH5........................40 C5
Orchard Wy *DORK* RH4...........40 B2
  KWD/TDW/WH KT20............24 A4
  REIG RH2 ....44 D2
Ormside Wy *REDH* RH1..........26 B5
Orpin Rd *REDH* RH1..............36 A3
Orwell Gdns *REIG* RH2...........44 D1
Osborne Rd *REDH* RH1..........35 E1
Oswald Cl *LHD/OX* KT22............9 E2
Oswald Rd *LHD/OX* KT22..........9 E2
Ottways Av *ASHTD* KT21..........3 H4
Ottways La *ASHTD* KT21...........4 A4
Outwood La
  KWD/TDW/WH KT20............14 D2
  REDH RH1 ....37 G2
Overdale *ASHTD* KT21.............4 A4
  RDKG RH5........................29 G5
  REDH RH1 ....37 E3
Oveton Wy *GT/LBKH* KT23.......18 C1
Owen Pl *LHD/OX* * KT22.........10 B2
Oxford Rd *REDH* RH1............34 C3
Oxshott Rd *LHD/OX* KT22..........2 D1

P

The Paddocks *GT/LBKH* KT23...18 D1
Paddocks Wy *ASHTD* KT21.......4 A3
The Paddock *DORK* RH4.........38 D2
Palmer Cl *HORL* RH6.............56 D1
  REDH RH1 ....35 E5
Paper Ms *DORK* RH4.............29 F5
The Parade
  KWD/TDW/WH * KT20...........7 E4
  LHD/OX * KT22....................3 F5
Park Av *REDH* RH1................53 H2
Park Cl *BRKHM/BTCW* RH3.......41 H4
  LHD/OX KT22......................9 F4
Park Copse *RDKG* RH5..........40 D1
Parker's Cl *ASHTD* KT21..........4 A4
Parker's HI *ASHTD* KT21...........4 A4
Parker's La *ASHTD* KT21..........4 B4
Parkgate Rd *REIG* RH2...........33 H5
Park Gn *GT/LBKH* KT23............8 C5
Park Hall Rd *REIG* RH2...........33 G2
Park House Dr *REIG* RH2.........44 B1

Parkhurst Gv *HORL* RH6 ....56 C2
Parkhurst Rd *HORL* RH6 ....56 C2
Parklands *GT/LBKH* KT23 ....8 C3
  RDKG RH5 ....40 B5
Park La *ASHTD* KT21.......................4 B3
  COUL/CHIP CR5 ....16 D1
  REIG RH2 ....33 F4
Park La East *REIG* RH2 ....44 B2
Parklawn Av *HORL* RH6 ....56 D1
Parkpale La *BRKHM/BTCW* RH3....41 G4
Park Ri *LHD/OX* KT22...................10 A1
Park Rise Cl *LHD/OX* KT22...........10 B1
Park Rd *ASHTD* KT21.......................4 A3
  REDH RH1 ....34 D2
The Park *GT/LBKH* KT23 ....8 C4
Park Vw *GT/LBKH* KT23 ....8 C4
  HORL RH6...................................57 E3
Park View Rd *REDH* RH1 ....54 A1
Park Wy *GT/LBKH* KT23 ....8 C3
Parkway *DORK* RH4.......................29 E5
Park Wy *GT/LBKH* KT23 ....8 C3
Parkwood Rd *REDH* RH1 ....36 A3
Park Wood Vw *BNSTD* SM7.............6 C1
Park Works Rd *REDH* RH1 ....36 B3
Parr Cl *LHD/OX* KT22......................2 D5
Parris Cft *RDKG* RH5 ....40 C4
Parsonage La *DORK* RH4..............39 E4
Parsonage Sq *DORK* RH4 ....29 E5
Parsons Cl *HORL* RH6...................56 C2
Parsonsfield Rd *BNSTD* SM7...........6 D1
Parthia Cl *KWD/TDW/WH* KT20......6 B4
Paul's Pl *ASHTD* KT21....................4 D4
The Pavement *REDH* * RH1............34 D4
Pear Tree Hl *REDH* * RH1..............54 A3
Pebble Cl *KWD/TDW/WH* KT20......22 C3
Pebblehill Rd
  BRKHM/BTCW RH3.....................22 C5
Pebble La *EPSOM* KT18 ....11 G2
Pelham Wy *GT/LBKH* KT23 ....18 D1
Pembroke Cl *BNSTD* SM7................7 H2
Pendell Ms *REDH* * RH1................34 D5
Pendell Rd *REDH* RH1 ....36 D1
Pendleton Cl *REDH* RH1 ....45 H1
Pendleton Rd *REDH* RH1 ....45 F2
Penrith Cl *REDH* RH1....................34 C3
Penrose Rd *LHD/OX* KT22...............9 C2
Pepys Cl *ASHTD* KT21....................4 E2
Perimeter Rd North *HORL* RH6 .....56 C5
Petersmead Cl
  KWD/TDW/WH KT20..................13 G3
Petridge Rd *REDH* RH1 ....45 H4
Petters Rd *ASHTD* KT21..................4 B1
Philanthropic Rd *REDH* RH1 ....35 E5
Picketts La *REDH* RH1...................54 C3
Picquets Wy *BNSTD* SM7................7 E1
Pigeonhouse La *COUL/CHIP* CR5....15 E5
Pilgrims Cl *RDKG* RH5 ....29 E2
Pilgrims' La *CTHM* CR3 ....27 F1
Pilgrims Pl *REIG* RH2 ....33 G2
Pilgrims Wy *RDKG* RH5 ....29 F1
  REIG RH2 ....33 F2
Pine Dean *GT/LBKH* KT23 ....8 D5
Pine Gdns *HORL* RH6....................57 E4
Pine Hl *EPSOM* KT18 ....5 F1
Pinehurst Cl
  KWD/TDW/WH KT20..................14 C2
Pine Wk *GT/LBKH* KT23 ....8 D5
Pippbrook Gdns *DORK* RH4 ....29 F5
Pit Wood Gn *KWD/TDW/WH* KT20...6 C5
Pixham La *DORK* RH4 ....29 G4
Pixholme Gv *DORK* RH4 ....29 G4
Pleasure Pit Rd *ASHTD* KT21 ....4 D3
Pointers Hl *DORK* RH4..................39 E3
The Pointers *ASHTD* KT21..............4 A5
Polesden Rd *GT/LBKH* KT23 ....18 D4
Polesden Vw *GT/LBKH* KT23 ....18 D2
Pond Farm Cl
  KWD/TDW/WH KT20..................13 F4
Poplar La *LHD/OX* KT22................10 B2
Poplar Rd *LHD/OX* KT22...............10 B2
Portland Dr *REDH* RH1 ....26 C4
Portland Rd *DORK* RH4.................29 E5
Post House La *GT/LBKH* KT23 ....8 C5
Potters Wy *REIG* RH2 ....45 E3
Pound Ct *ASHTD* KT21...................4 D4
Pound Crs *LHD/OX* KT22................9 F1
Pound Rd *BNSTD* SM7....................7 G2
Povey Cross Rd *HORL* RH6............56 B5
Powell Cl *HORL* RH6.....................56 C1
Poynes Rd *HORL* RH6...................56 C1
Premier Pde *HORL* * RH6.............57 F3
Preston Gv *ASHTD* KT21.................3 G2
Preston La *KWD/TDW/WH* KT20.....6 C5
Pretty La *COUL/CHIP* CR5.............16 B1
Prices La *REIG* RH2.......................44 C2
Primrose Av *HORL* RH6.................57 F5
Prince Albert Sq *REDH* RH1..........45 H4
Prince of Wales Rd *REDH* RH1......55 G2
Prince's Rd *REDH* RH1..................45 H1

Princess Wy *REDH* RH1.................35 E3
Priors Md *GT/LBKH* KT23................9 E5
The Priors *ASHTD* KT21...................3 H4
Priory Cl *DORK* RH4 ....40 A3
  HORL RH6...................................56 D2
Priory Ct *DORK* * RH4...................40 B3
Priory Dr *REIG* RH2......................44 C1
Priory Rd *REIG* RH2......................44 C1
Proctor Gdns *GT/LBKH* KT23 ....8 D5
Prossers *KWD/TDW/WH* KT20 ......13 H1
Punchbowl La *RDKG* RH5 ....29 H5
Purbeck Cl *REDH* RH1 ....26 C4

Q

Quality St *REDH* RH1.....................26 B3
Quarry Cl *LHD/OX* KT22................10 D1
Quarry Cl *LHD/OX* KT22................10 D1
Quarry Hill Pk *REIG* RH2..............34 A1
The Quarry *BRKHM/BTCW* RH3.....31 F2
Queen Annes Ms *LHD/OX* * KT22...10 B1
Queen Anne's Ter
  LHD/OX * KT22..........................10 B1
Queens Cl *KWD/TDW/WH* KT20 ...13 E4
Queens Crs *DORK* * RH4...............40 A2
Queens Rd *HORL* RH6...................57 E3
Queensway *REDH* RH1..................34 D3
Quennell Cl *ASHTD* KT21................4 B4

R

Radolphs *KWD/TDW/WH* KT20.......13 H1
Radstock Wy *REDH* RH1................26 D3
Raglan Cl *REIG* RH2......................34 A2
Raglan Rd *REIG* RH2.....................33 H2
Ralliwood Rd *ASHTD* KT21 ....4 C4
Ralphs Cross *GT/LBKH* * KT23 .....19 E1
Ramsey Cl *HORL* RH6....................56 D3
Randal Crs *REIG* RH2....................44 C1
Randalls Crs *LHD/OX* KT22.............3 E5
Randalls Park Av *LHD/OX* KT22......3 E5
Randalls Park Dr *LHD/OX* KT22 ...10 A1
Randalls Rd *LHD/OX* KT22..............2 C5
Randalls Wy *LHD/OX* KT22...........10 A1
Ranelagh Rd *REDH* RH1................34 C4
Ranmore Cl *REDH* RH1 ....35 E1
Ranmore Common Rd
  RDKG RH5 ....28 B3
Ranmore Rd *RDKG* RH5 ....28 C4
Rathgar Cl *REDH* RH1...................46 A4
Ravens Cl *REDH* RH1....................34 D3
Raymead Cl *LHD/OX* KT22..............9 G2
Raymead Wy *LHD/OX* KT22............9 G2
Raymer Wk *HORL* RH6..................57 G2
Reading Arch Rd *REDH* RH1..........34 D4
Read Rd *ASHTD* KT21.....................3 H2
Reads Rest La
  KWD/TDW/WH KT20....................7 F4
Rectory Cl *ASHTD* KT21 ....4 B4
Rectory La *ASHTD* KT21..................4 B3
  BRKHM/BTCW RH3.....................31 H2
  GT/LBKH KT23...........................18 B1
Rectory Rd *COUL/CHIP* CR5..........15 F5
Redcote Pl *DORK* RH4...................29 H4
Redlands La *RDKG* RH5.................48 A2
Red La *RDKG* RH5.........................49 G1
Redstone Hl *REDH* RH1.................35 E3
Redstone Hollow *REDH* RH1..........35 E5
Redstone Mnr *REDH* RH1..............35 E4
Redstone Pk *REDH* RH1................35 E4
Redstone Rd *REDH* RH1................35 E5
Redwood Mt *REIG* RH2..................33 G1
Reed Dr *REDH* RH1.......................46 A2
Reeve Rd *REDH* RH1.....................45 E3
Regent Cl *REDH* RH1....................26 C4
Regent Crs *REDH* RH1..................34 D2
Regent Pk *LHD/OX* * KT22..............3 E5
Regents Ms *HORL* RH6..................57 E3
Reigate Hl *REIG* RH2....................24 D5
Reigate Hill Cl *REIG* RH2..............33 G1
Reigate Rd *BRKHM/BTCW* RH3.....31 E3
  DORK RH4 ....30 A4
  EPSOM KT18 ....6 D2
  HORL RH6...................................53 E4
  HORL RH6...................................56 B4
  LHD/OX KT22.............................10 C3
  REIG RH2 ....34 A4
The Renmans *ASHTD* KT21.............4 B1
Rennie Ter *REDH* RH1...................35 E5
Revell Cl *LHD/OX* KT22...................8 D2
Revell Dr *LHD/OX* KT22...................8 D2
Richbell Cl *ASHTD* KT21..................3 H3
Richmond Cl *GT/LBKH* KT23............9 E4
Richmond Wy *GT/LBKH* KT23..........8 D3

Rickwood *HORL* RH6.....................57 F2
Ridge Cl *BRKHM/BTCW* RH3.........41 H3
Ridgegate Cl *REIG* RH2.................34 B2
Ridge Gn *REDH* RH1......................47 E2
Ridge Green Cl *REDH* RH1.............47 E2
Ridgelands *LHD/OX* KT22................9 F4
Ridgemount Wy *REDH* RH1...........45 F1
The Ridge *REDH* KT18.....................5 E3
  LHD/OX KT22...............................9 F4
Ridgeway Cl *DORK* RH4.................40 A3
Ridgeway Ct *REDH* * RH1..............34 C5
Ridgeway Dr *DORK* RH4................40 A3
Ridgeway Rd *DORK* RH4................40 A3
  REDH RH1 ....34 D4
The Ridgeway *HORL* RH6..............57 E5
  LHD/OX KT22...............................9 F3
The Ridings *ASHTD* KT21................3 H2
  KWD/TDW/WH KT20....................7 F5
  REDH RH1 ....34 B2
Ringley Av *HORL* RH6...................57 E4
Ringley Park Av *REIG* RH2............34 B5
Ringley Park Rd *REIG* RH2............34 A4
Ringwood Av *REDH* RH1................34 D1
The Rise *KWD/TDW/WH* KT20.......13 G1
Riverbank *DORK* * RH4..................38 D1
River La *LHD/OX* KT22....................2 B5
Riverside *DORK* RH4.....................29 H4
  HORL RH6...................................57 E5
Robin Gdns *REDH* RH1..................35 E2
Rockshaw Rd *REDH* RH1...............26 C2
Rocky La *REIG* RH2.......................26 A4
Roebuck Cl *ASHTD* KT21.................4 A5
  REIG RH2 ....33 H3
Roffey Cl *HORL* RH6......................56 D3
Roman Rd *DORK* RH4....................40 A1
Ronson Wy *LHD/OX* KT22..............10 A1
Rookery Cl *LHD/OX* KT22................9 G4
Rookery Dr *DORK* RH4...................38 C3
Rookery Hl *ASHTD* KT21..................4 C3
  REDH RH1 ....55 H5
Rookery Wy
  KWD/TDW/WH KT20..................24 B2
Rook La *CTHM* CR3.......................17 G4
Rookwood Cl *REDH* RH1................26 B4
Roothill La *BRKHM/BTCW* RH3.....41 G5
Rosebank Cottages *REIG* * RH2 ....44 D1
Roseberry Rd *EPSOM* KT18.............5 G4
Rose Bushes *EW* KT17....................6 C1
Rosedale *ASHTD* KT21....................3 G3
Rose Hl *DORK* RH4.......................40 A1
Rose Hill Arch Ms *DORK* * RH4.....40 A1
Rosemary Ct *HORL* * RH6..............56 C2
Rosemary La *HORL* RH6................56 C2
Rosemead Cl *REDH* RH1...............45 F1
Roses Cottages *DORK* * RH4.........40 A1
Rothervale *HORL* RH6...................56 D1
Rothes Rd *DORK* RH4...................29 F5
Rough Rew *RDKG* RH5..................40 B4
Rowan Cl *REIG* RH2.......................45 E1
Rowan Gv *COUL/CHIP* CR5...........16 B5
Rowan Md *KWD/TDW/WH* KT20.....6 B4
Royal Dr *EPSOM* KT18....................6 B3
Royal Earlswood Pk *REDH* RH1.....46 A3
Ruffetts Wy *KWD/TDW/WH* KT20...7 E3
Rural Wy *REDH* RH1......................35 E4
Rushett Dr *DORK* RH4...................40 B4
Rushetts Rd *REIG* RH2..................45 E3
Rushworth Rd *REIG* RH2...............33 G3
Russell Cl *KWD/TDW/WH* KT20....13 E5
Russell Ct *LHD/OX* KT22...............10 B2
Russells *KWD/TDW/WH* KT20 ......13 H2
Russells Crs *HORL* RH6.................57 G3
Russet Cl *HORL* RH6.....................57 G3
Russet Wy *RDKG* RH5...................40 D4
Rutherwick Cl *HORL* RH6..............56 D3
Rutland Cl *ASHTD* KT21..................4 A2
  REDH RH1 ....34 D3
Rye Brook Rd *LHD/OX* KT22...........3 E3
Ryelands *HORL* * RH6...................57 G2
Ryelands Ct *LHD/OX* KT22..............3 E3

S

Saddlers Wy *EPSOM* KT18 ....5 F4
St Alban's Rd *REIG* RH2................33 G2
St Andrews *HORL* * RH6................57 F4
St Andrew's Cl *REIG* RH2..............33 H5
St Annes Bvd *REDH* RH1...............35 E3
St Anne's Dr *REDH* RH1................35 E3
St Annes Mt *REDH* * RH1..............35 E3
St Annes Ri *REDH* RH1..................35 E3
St Annes Wy *REDH* * RH1.............35 E3
St Aubyns *DORK* * RH4.................40 B3
St Brelades Cl *DORK* RH4.............40 A3
St Catherine's Cross *REDH* RH1....37 G4
St Clair Cl *REIG* RH2.....................34 A4

St David's Cl *REIG* RH2.................34
St Georges *HORL* * RH6................57
St Georges Cl *HORL* RH6..............57
St George's Rd *REDH* RH1.............54
St Hilda's Cl *REDH* RH6................57
St John's *RDKG* RH5.....................40
St John's Av *LHD/OX* KT22............10
St John's Cl *LHD/OX* KT22............10
St John's Rd *DORK* RH4................39
  LHD/OX KT22.............................10
  REDH RH1 45
St John's Ter Rd *REDH* RH1..........34
St Leonards Rd
  KWD/TDW/WH KT20..................10
St Margaret's Rd
  COUL/CHIP CR5.........................16
St Marks Rd *EPSOM* KT18...............6
St Martins Ms *DORK* RH4..............40
St Mary's Cl *LHD/OX* KT22..............9
St Marys Rd *LHD/OX* KT22............10
  REIG RH2 33
St Matthew's Rd *REDH* RH1..........34
St Monica's Rd
  KWD/TDW/WH KT20.....................1
St Nicholas Av *GT/LBKH* KT23........1
St Nicholas Hl *LHD/OX* KT22.........10
St Paul's Rd East *DORK* RH4..........40
St Paul's Rd West *DORK* RH4........40
St Stephens Av *ASHTD* KT21...........1
Salbrook Rd *REDH* RH1.................54
Salvation Pl *LHD/OX* KT22............10
Sandcross La *REIG* RH2.................44
Sandes Pl *LHD/OX* KT22................44
Sandhills Rd *REIG* RH2..................44
Sandlands Gv
  KWD/TDW/WH KT20....................13
Sandlands Rd
  KWD/TDW/WH KT20....................13
Sandpit Rd *REDH* RH1...................34
Sandrock Rd *DORK* RH4................38
Sandy La *BRKHM/BTCW* RH3........31
  KWD/TDW/WH KT20....................14
  REDH RH1 35
  REDH RH1 35
  REIG RH2 32
Sangers Dr *HORL* RH6..................56
Sarel Wy *HORL* RH6......................57
Saxley *HORL* RH6..........................57
Saxons *KWD/TDW/WH* KT20.........13
Saxon Wy *REIG* RH2......................34
Sayers Cl *LHD/OX* KT22..................9
School Hl *REDH* RH1......................26
School La *DORK* RH4.....................39
  LHD/OX KT22...............................9
  RDKG RH5 20
Searle Hl *REIG* RH2.......................44
Shabden Cottages
  COUL/CHIP * CR5......................15
Shamrock Cl *LHD/OX* KT22.............8
Sharon Cl *GT/LBKH* KT23................8
Shaw Gv *KWD/TDW/WH* KT20......14
Shawley Crs *EPSOM* KT18...............6
Shawley Wy *EPSOM* KT18...............6
Sheephouse Gn *RDKG* RH5............38
Sheephouse La *RDKG* RH5............38
Sheep Wk *REIG* RH2......................33
Sheldon Cl *REIG* RH2.....................33
Shellwood Dr *RDKG* RH5...............40
Shellwood Rd *REIG* RH2................50
Shelvers Gn
  KWD/TDW/WH KT20....................13
Shelvers Hl *KWD/TDW/WH* KT20...13
Shelvers Spur
  KWD/TDW/WH KT20....................13
Shelvers Wy
  KWD/TDW/WH KT20....................13
Shepherd's Hl *REDH* RH1..............26
Shepherds' Wk *EPSOM* KT18........11
Sherborne Cl *EPSOM* KT18.............6
Shere Cl *RDKG* RH5......................40
Sheridan Dr *REIG* RH2..................33
Sheridans Rd *GT/LBKH* KT23.........19
Sherwood Cl *LHD/OX* KT22.............8
Sherwood Crs *REIG* RH2...............44
Shire Pl *REDH* RH1........................45
Shirley Av *REDH* RH1....................34
Shortacres *REDH* RH1...................36
Shrewsbury Rd *REDH* RH1.............34
Shrubland Rd *BNSTD* SM7...............7
Sideways La *HORL* RH6.................56
Silver Cl *KWD/TDW/WH* KT20.......14
Silverdale Cl
  BRKHM/BTCW RH3.....................41
Silverlea Gdns *HORL* RH6.............56
Silverstone Cl *REDH* RH1..............34
Sincots Rd *REDH* RH1...................34
Skinners La *ASHTD* KT21...............3
Skipton Wy *HORL* RH6..................57

...natch Rd *REIG* RH2 ....44 B3
...hoe St *REIG* RH2 ....33 F4
...gh La *BRKHM/BTCW* RH3 ....32 A3
...SOM KT18 ....12 A5
...tfield Rd *HORL* RH6 ....57 F3
...lmead *HORL* RH6 ....57 F3
...ls Hill Rd *REIG* RH6 ....51 G4
...nbarn Ct *HORL* RH6 ....57 F2
...Smithers
...KHM/BTCW RH3 ....41 H1
...n Rd *REIG* RH2 ....44 B2
...hy La *KWD/TDW/WH* KT20 ...24 B1
...hy La *KWD/TDW/WH* KT20 ...24 B1
...urge La *REIG* RH2 ....44 D1
...verhill Rd
...KHM/BTCW RH3 ....42 D3
...cote *GT/LBKH* KT23 ....8 C5
...Farm Av *GT/LBKH* KT23 ....8 B5
...Farm Cl *GT/LBKH* KT23 ....8 B4
...Farm Rd *GT/LBKH* KT23 ....8 B5
...erfield Cl
...D/TDW/WH KT20 ....7 E4
...ers Cl *REIG* RH2 ....33 G3
...erset Rd *REIG* RH2 ....45 F1
...ers Rd *REIG* RH2 ....33 G3
...les Farm *DORK* RH4 ....39 H1
...les Place Cottages
...RK * RH4 ....39 H1
...les Place Dr *DORK* RH4 ....39 H1
...n Albert Rd *REIG* RH2 ....33 F3
...n Close Gn *REIG* RH2 ....33 G3
...ncote Rd *REDH* RH1 ....26 C5
...n Dr *RDKG* RH5 ....48 D1
...n End *GT/LBKH* KT23 ....18 D1
...hern Av *REDH* RH1 ....54 A1
...herns La *COUL/CHIP* CR5 .....15 E4
...hlands Av *HORL* RH6 ....57 E2
...n Md *REDH* RH1 ....34 D1
...n Pde *HORL* * RH6 ....56 D2
...DH * RH1 ....26 C3
...n Rd *REIG* RH2 ....33 H5
...n Station Ap *REDH* RH1 ....47 F1
...n St *DORK* RH4 ....40 A2
...n Ter *DORK* RH4 ....40 B2
...n View Rd *ASHTD* KT21 ....3 H4
...n Wk *REIG* * RH2 ....33 H4
...rows Md *REDH* RH1 ....35 E1
...cer Cl *EPSOM* KT18 ....5 C4
...cer Wy *REDH* RH1 ....46 A4
...rs Wy *HORL* RH6 ....57 F5
...dlewoods
...D/TDW/WH KT20 ....13 F2
...Spinney *EPSOM* KT18 ....6 B4
...LBKH KT23 ....8 D4
...RL RH6 ....57 F3
...al Heath *RDKG* RH5 ....29 C5
...k HI *RDKG* RH5 ....48 B1
...ngcopse Rd *REIG* RH2 ....34 A5
...ngfield Rd *DORK* RH4 ....38 D2
...ng Gv *GT/LBKH* KT23 ....8 D3
...n Dr *KWD/TDW/WH* KT20 .....14 D1
...rrels Gn *GT/LBKH* KT23 ....8 C2
...fords Pl *HORL* RH6 ....57 F4
...Leys *ASHTD* KT21 ....4 A5
...hs Wy *KWD/TDW/WH* KT20 ....6 B5
...ehurst Cl *REDH* RH1 ....45 E3
...ehurst Rd *REDH* RH1 ....45 E3
...La *COUL/CHIP* CR5 ....16 A1
...on Ap *DORK* RH4 ....29 G4
...RL RH6 ....57 F3
...on Ap East *REDH* RH1 ....45 H1
...on Approach Rd
...D/TDW/WH KT20 ....13 G2
...on Ap West *REDH* RH1 ....45 H1
...on Rd *BRKHM/BTCW* RH3 .....31 F3
...RK RH4 ....28 D5
...RL RH6 ....57 F3
...D/OX KT22 ....10 A1
...DH RH1 ....26 C3
...DH RH1 ....34 C3
...on Rd North *REDH* RH1 ....26 C3
...on Rd South *REDH* RH1 ....26 C3
...on Yd
...D/TDW/WH * KT20 ....14 B1
...art *KWD/TDW/WH* KT20 ....13 H1
...ng Cl *BNSTD* SM7 ....7 F2
...kfield *HORL* * RH6 ....57 F2
...ks Cl *HORL* RH6 ....57 F4
...D/OX KT22 ....10 A1
...DH RH1 ....26 C3
...DH RH1 ....34 C3
...on Rd North *REDH* RH1 ....26 C3
...on Rd South *REDH* RH1 ....26 C3
...on Yd
...D/TDW/WH * KT20 ....14 B1
...ecourt Cl *HORL* RH6 ....57 G3
...ehill Cl *GT/LBKH* KT23 ....8 C5

Stones La *DORK* RH4 ....39 E2
Stoney Cft *COUL/CHIP* CR5 ......16 C2
Stonny Cft *ASHTD* KT21 ....4 B3
Strand Cl *EPSOM* KT18 ....5 F1
Strathcona Av *EHSLY* KT24 ....18 A3
The Street *ASHTD* KT21 ....4 B3
 BRKHM/BTCW RH3 ....31 F4
 LHD/OX KT22 ....9 F2
Stuart Crs *REIG* RH2 ....44 C2
Stuart Rd *REIG* RH2 ....44 C2
Stubbs La *KWD/TDW/WH* KT20 .24 B5
Stubs Cl *DORK* RH4 ....40 C3
Stubs HI *DORK* RH4 ....40 C3
Sturt's La *KWD/TDW/WH* KT20 ..22 D2
Stychens Cl *REDH* RH1 ....37 E3
Stychens La *REDH* RH1 ....37 E3
Styles End *GT/LBKH* KT23 ....18 D2
Subrosa Dr *REDH* RH1 ....26 B5
Subrosa Pk *REDH* * RH1 ....26 B5
Suffolk Cl *HORL* RH6 ....57 E4
Summerfield *ASHTD* KT21 ....3 H4
Summerlay Cl
 KWD/TDW/WH KT20 ....14 A1
Summerly Av *REIG* RH2 ....33 G3
Sumner Cl *LHD/OX* KT22 ....9 F2
Sunmead Cl *LHD/OX* KT22 ....9 F2
Sunmead Pde *LHD/OX* * KT22 ...14 A2
Sunny Bank *EPSOM* KT18 ....5 E1
Surrey Hills Av
 KWD/TDW/WH KT20 ....31 E1
Surrey Hills Wy
 KWD/TDW/WH KT20 ....22 A5
Sussex Cl *HORL* RH6 ....34 B5
Sutton Gdns *REDH* RH1 ....26 A4
Swallow La *RDKG* RH5 ....48 B2
Swan Mill Gdns *DORK* RH4 ....29 G4
Swanns Meadow
 GT/LBKH KT23 ....18 C1
Swanworth La *RDKG* RH5 ....20 B3
Sycamore Cl *LHD/OX* KT22 ....9 F4
Sycamore Wk *REIG* RH2 ....45 E2
Sylvan Wy *REDH* RH1 ....35 E5

T

Tabarin Wy *EW* KT17 ....6 C1
Tadorne Rd
 KWD/TDW/WH KT20 ....13 G1
Tadworth Cl
 KWD/TDW/WH KT20 ....13 H2
Tadworth St
 KWD/TDW/WH KT20 ....13 G3
Talbot Cl *REIG* RH2 ....33 H5
Taleworth Cl *ASHTD* KT21 ....3 H5
Taleworth Pk *ASHTD* KT21 ....3 H5
Taleworth Rd *ASHTD* KT21 ....3 H4
Talisman Wy *EW* KT17 ....6 C1
Tangier Wy *KWD/TDW/WH* KT20 ..7 E2
Tangier Wd *KWD/TDW/WH* KT20 ..7 E3
Tanners Dean *LHD/OX* KT22 ......10 D2
Tanner's HI *BRKHM/BTCW* RH3 ...41 H1
Tanners Meadow
 BRKHM/BTCW RH3 ....41 H3
The Tannery *REDH* RH1 ....34 C4
Tanyard Wy *HORL* RH6 ....57 F2
Tapner's Rd *REIG* RH2 ....42 D5
Tarham Cl *HORL* RH6 ....56 C1
Tate Cl *LHD/OX* KT22 ....10 C3
Tattenham Corner Rd
 EPSOM KT18 ....5 H2
Tattenham Crs *EPSOM* KT18 ....6 A3
Tattenham Gv *EPSOM* KT18 ....6 B3
Tattenham Wy
 KWD/TDW/WH KT20 ....13 H2
Taylor Rd *ASHTD* KT21 ....3 H2
Taynton Dr *REDH* RH1 ....26 D5
Teal Ct *DORK* * RH4 ....29 E5
Teazlewood Pk *LHD/OX* KT22 ......3 E2
Temple Wood Dr *REDH* * RH1 ...34 D1
Ten Acres Cl *LHD/OX* KT22 ....9 F4
Thames Down Link *ASHTD* KT21 ...4 C1
Thatchers Cl *HORL* RH6 ....57 F1
Thepps Cl *REDH* RH1 ....47 F2
Thornton Cl *HORL* RH6 ....56 C3
Thornton Pl *HORL* RH6 ....56 C3
Three Arches Pk *REDH* * RH1 ....45 H3
Three Arch Rd *REDH* RH1 ....46 A3
Thurnham Wy
 KWD/TDW/WH KT20 ....13 H3
Tilehurst La *RDKG* RH5 ....41 E2
Tiler's Wy *REDH* RH1 ....45 E3
Tilgate Common *REDH* RH1 ....37 E3
Tilley La *EPSOM* KT18 ....12 A3
Timber Cl *GT/LBKH* KT23 ....19 E2
Timber HI *ASHTD* KT21 ....4 A4
Timperley Gdns *REDH* RH1 ....34 C2

Todds Cl *HORL* RH6 ....56 C1
Tollgate Av *REDH* RH1 ....45 H4
Tollgate Rd *DORK* RH4 ....40 B4
The Topiary *ASHTD* KT21 ....4 A5
Tower Cl *HORL* RH6 ....56 D3
Tower HI *DORK* RH4 ....40 B3
Tower Hill Rd *DORK* RH4 ....40 B3
Tower Rd *KWD/TDW/WH* KT20 ...13 G3
Townfield Rd *DORK* RH4 ....40 A2
Town Md *REDH* RH1 ....37 F3
Townshott Cl *GT/LBKH* KT23 .....18 C1
Tranquil Dl *BRKHM/BTCW* RH3 ...31 H2
Trasher Md *RDKG* RH5 ....40 D4
Treadwell Rd *EPSOM* KT18 ....5 G1
Treelands *RDKG* RH5 ....40 C4
Tree View Ct *REIG* * RH2 ....34 B4
Treeway *REIG* RH2 ....33 H1
Tregarthen Pl *LHD/OX* KT22 ......10 C1
Trehaven Pde *REIG* RH2 ....44 D2
Trentham Rd *REDH* RH1 ....45 H1
Trindles Rd *REDH* RH1 ....47 F1
Trittons *KWD/TDW/WH* KT20 ....13 G1
Trowers Wy *REDH* RH1 ....35 F1
Trumpetshill Rd *REIG* RH2 ....32 A5
Tudor Cl *GT/LBKH* KT23 ....8 A4
The Tudors *REIG* * RH2 ....34 A1
Tudor Wk *LHD/OX* KT22 ....3 E5
Tulyar Cl *KWD/TDW/WH* KT20 .....6 B4
Tumber St *EPSOM* KT18 ....12 A5
Tumblewood Rd *BNSTD* SM7 ......7 E1
Tweed La *BRKHM/BTCW* RH3 ....41 H3
Twelve Acre Cl *GT/LBKH* KT23 .....8 D3
Twyner Cl *HORL* RH6 ....57 G2
Tynedale Rd *BRKHM/BTCW* RH3 ..41 H3

U

Underhill Park Rd *REIG* RH2 ....33 G1
Upfield *HORL* RH6 ....57 E4
Upfield Cl *HORL* RH6 ....57 E5
Uplands *ASHTD* KT21 ....3 H5
Upland Wy *EPSOM* KT18 ....6 C3
Upper Bridge Rd *REDH* RH1 ......34 C4
Upper Fairfield Rd
 LHD/OX KT22 ....10 B1
Upper Kiln *DORK* * RH4 ....40 C3
Upper Pth *DORK* * RH4 ....40 C3
Upper Rose Hl *DORK* RH4 ....40 B2
Upper West St *REIG* RH2 ....33 F4
Usherwood Cl
 KWD/TDW/WH KT20 ....31 E1

V

Vandyke Cl *REDH* RH1 ....34 D2
Vaughan Wy *DORK* RH4 ....40 A1
Vernon Wk *KWD/TDW/WH* KT20 ..6 D5
Vevers Rd *REIG* RH2 ....44 D2
Vicarage Cl *GT/LBKH* KT23 ....8 C5
 KWD/TDW/WH KT20 ....14 A4
Vicarage Gate Ms
 KWD/TDW/WH KT20 ....14 A4
Vicarage La *HORL* RH6 ....56 D2
 LHD/OX KT22 ....10 B2
Victoria Cl *HORL* RH6 ....57 E3
Victoria Rd *HORL* RH6 ....57 E3
 REDH RH1 ....35 E5
Victoria Ter *DORK* * RH4 ....40 A1
Vincent Cl *GT/LBKH* KT23 ....8 D3
Vincent Dr *DORK* RH4 ....40 A2
Vincent La *DORK* RH4 ....40 A1
Vincent Rd *DORK* RH4 ....40 A1
Vincent Wk *DORK* * RH4 ....40 A1
Virginia Cl *ASHTD* KT21 ....3 H3
Vogan Cl *REIG* RH2 ....44 D2

W

Walford Rd *RDKG* RH5 ....40 B5
Walkfield Dr *EPSOM* KT18 ....6 B2
Wallace Sq *COUL/CHIP* CR5 ......16 D2
The Walled Gdn
 BRKHM/BTCW RH3 ....31 F5
Wallis Ms *LHD/OX* * KT22 ....10 A2
Walnut Dr *KWD/TDW/WH* KT20 ..14 A4
Walter's Md *ASHTD* KT21 ....4 A2
Walton Rd *EPSOM* KT18 ....12 A1
Walton St *KWD/TDW/WH* KT20 ..13 E4
Wanmer Ct *REIG* * RH2 ....33 G3
The Waplings
 KWD/TDW/WH * KT20 ....13 F4
Warenne Hts *REDH* RH1 ....45 F1

Warenne Rd *LHD/OX* KT22 ....9 E2
Warltersville Wy *HORL* RH6 ....57 G5
Warren Dr *KWD/TDW/WH* KT20 ..14 B2
Warren HI *EPSOM* KT18 ....5 F1
Warren Lodge Dr
 KWD/TDW/WH KT20 ....14 A4
Warrenne Rd
 BRKHM/BTCW RH3 ....42 A2
Warrenne Wy *REIG* RH2 ....33 G4
Warren Pk
 KWD/TDW/WH KT20 ....31 E1
Warren Rd *REIG* RH2 ....33 H3
The Warren *ASHTD* KT21 ....4 B5
 KWD/TDW/WH KT20 ....14 A3
Warwick Cl *RDKG* RH5 ....48 B4
Warwick Gdns *ASHTD* KT21 ....3 G2
Warwick Rd *RDKG* RH5 ....48 C5
 REDH RH1 ....34 D3
Warwick Wold Rd *REDH* RH1 .....27 G4
Washington Cl *REIG* RH2 ....33 G2
Wasp Green La *REDH* RH1 ....55 H3
Waterer Gdns
 KWD/TDW/WH KT20 ....7 E3
Waterfield Cl
 KWD/TDW/WH KT20 ....6 B4
Waterfield Gn
 KWD/TDW/WH KT20 ....6 B5
Waterfields *LHD/OX* KT22 ....3 E4
Waterhouse La
 KWD/TDW/WH KT20 ....14 A1
 REDH RH1 ....37 H2
Water La *GT/LBKH* KT23 ....18 A1
Waterlow Rd *REIG* RH2 ....34 A5
Watermead *KWD/TDW/WH* KT20 .13 F1
Waterside *HORL* RH6 ....57 E1
Waterslade *REDH* RH1 ....34 C4
Waterway Rd *LHD/OX* KT22 ......10 A2
Wathen Rd *DORK* RH4 ....29 F5
Watson Rd *DORK* RH4 ....39 E2
Watts Cl *KWD/TDW/WH* * KT20 ..13 H2
Watt's La *KWD/TDW/WH* KT20 ...13 H2
Watt's Md *KWD/TDW/WH* KT20 ..13 H2
Waverley Pl *LHD/OX* * KT22 ......10 B2
The Way *REIG* RH2 ....34 B3
Weald Wy *REIG* RH2 ....45 E3
Weldon Wy *REDH* RH1 ....26 D4
Wellesford Cl *BNSTD* SM7 ....7 F2
Wellhouse La
 BRKHM/BTCW RH3 ....42 B2
Wellington Wy *HORL* RH6 ....56 D1
Wells Cl *GT/LBKH* KT23 ....8 D4
Wells Pl *REDH* RH1 ....26 B5
Wenlock Edge *DORK* * RH4 ......40 C3
Wesley Cl *HORL* RH6 ....57 E1
 REIG RH2 ....33 F5
Wessels *KWD/TDW/WH* KT20 ....13 H1
West Av *REDH* RH1 ....45 H5
West Bank *DORK* RH4 ....39 H2
Westcott Rd *DORK* RH4 ....39 H1
Westcott St *DORK* RH4 ....38 D2
West Down *GT/LBKH* KT23 ....18 D2
West Dr *KWD/TDW/WH* KT20 .....6 B2
Western Pl *DORK* * RH4 ....40 A1
West Farm Av *ASHTD* KT21 ....3 G3
West Farm Cl *ASHTD* KT21 ....3 G4
West Farm Dr *ASHTD* KT21 ....3 H4
Westfield *REIG* RH2 ....33 H1
Westfield Dr *GT/LBKH* KT23 ....8 D2
Westhumble St *RDKG* RH5 ....29 F1
Westleas *HORL* RH6 ....56 C1
Westlees Cl *RDKG* RH5 ....40 C4
West Md *HORL* RH6 ....57 G3
Westmead Dr *REDH* RH1 ....54 A2
West Rd *REIG* RH2 ....33 H5
West St *DORK* RH4 ....40 A1
 REIG RH2 ....33 F4
Westview Cl *REDH* RH1 ....45 G2
Westway Gdns *REDH* RH1 ....35 E1
Wheatfield Wy *HORL* RH6 ....57 E2
Wheelers La *BRKHM/BTCW* RH3 ..41 H1
Whitebeam Dr *REIG* RH2 ....45 E2
White Beam Wy
 KWD/TDW/WH KT20 ....13 E1
White Bushes *REDH* RH1 ....46 A3
Whitegate Wy
 KWD/TDW/WH KT20 ....6 B5
Whitehall La *REIG* RH2 ....44 B3
White HI *COUL/CHIP* CR5 ....15 F3
White Lodge Gdns *REDH* RH1 ....54 A2
Whitepost HI *REDH* RH1 ....34 C4
White Wy *GT/LBKH* KT23 ....18 D1
Whitmore Wy *HORL* RH6 ....56 D2
Wickham Cl *HORL* RH6 ....56 D2
Wiggie La *REDH* RH1 ....35 E2
Wildcroft Dr *RDKG* RH5 ....40 D4
Wiley Broom La *CTHM* CR3 ....17 E1
William Evelyn Ct *RDKG* * RH5 ...38 B4
Willowbank Gdns
 KWD/TDW/WH KT20 ....13 F2

Willow Brean *HORL* RH6 ....56 C2
Willow Ct *HORL* * RH6 ....54 B5
Willow Md *DORK* RH4 ....29 E5
Willow Rd *REDH* RH1....................45 E2
Willow V *GT/LBKH* KT23 ....8 D3
Willow Wk *KWD/TDW/WH* KT20 ...21 H5
  REDH RH1 ....46 B1
Wilmerhatch La *EPSOM* KT18 ....4 D2
Wilmots Cl *REIG* RH2....................34 A3
Wilsons *KWD/TDW/WH* KT20 ......13 H1
Wilton Rd *REDH* RH1....................34 D5
Wimborne Av *REDH* RH1...............45 H4
Windermere Wy *REDH* RH1...........34 C3
Windmill Cl *HORL* RH6 ....57 F3
Windmill Dr *LHD/OX* KT22............10 B3
  REDH RH1 ....34 B2
Windmill Wy *REDH* RH1................34 B2
Wither Dl *HORL* RH6 ....56 C2
Withey Brook *HORL* RH6 ....56 B5
Withey Mdw *HORL* RH6 ....56 B5
The Withies *LHD/OX* KT22..............3 F5
Withybed Cnr
  KWD/TDW/WH KT20...................13 F3
Wolvens La *DORK* RH4 ....38 C5
Wolverton Cl *HORL* RH6 ....56 D5
Wolverton Gdns *HORL* RH6 ....56 D4
Wonford Cl *KWD/TDW/WH* KT20 ...23 E1
Wonham La *BRKHM/BTCW* RH3 ....31 H5
Woodbridge Av *LHD/OX* KT22 ....3 E3
Woodbridge Gv *LHD/OX* KT22 ....3 E3
Wood Cl *REDH* RH1......................54 A3
Woodcote *HORL* RH6 ....57 F2
Woodcote Green Rd
  EPSOM KT18 ....5 E1
Woodcote Hurst *EPSOM* KT18........5 E1
Woodcote Park Rd *EPSOM* KT18.....5 E1

Woodcote Side *EPSOM* KT18 ....5 E1
Woodcrest Wk *REDH* RH1 ....34 C2
Woodend *LHD/OX* KT22 ....10 C5
Woodfield *ASHTD* KT21 ....3 H2
Woodfield Cl *ASHTD* KT21 ....3 H2
  REDH RH1 ....34 C3
Woodfield La *ASHTD* KT21 ....4 A1
Woodfield Rd *ASHTD* KT21 ....3 H2
Woodfield Wy *REDH* RH1 ....34 C3
Woodgavil *BNSTD* SM7 ....7 F1
Woodhatch Rd *REDH* RH1 ....45 F3
Woodhayes *HORL* RH6 ....56 F2
Woodlands *ASHTD* * KT21...............4 B3
Woodlands Av *REDH* RH1..............34 D5
Woodlands Copse *ASHTD* KT21 ......3 H1
Woodlands Ct *REDH* * RH1............45 H1
Woodlands Gdns *EPSOM* KT18 ....6 C2
Woodlands Pk
  KWD/TDW/WH KT20...................30 D1
Woodlands Rd *EHSLY* KT24 ....18 B3
  LHD/OX KT22 ....2 B3
  REDH RH1 ....45 H1
Woodlands Wy *ASHTD* KT21............4 C1
  KWD/TDW/WH KT20...................22 A5
Woodland Wy
  KWD/TDW/WH KT20...................14 A2
Wood La *KWD/TDW/WH* KT20........7 F2
Woodroyd Av *HORL* RH6 ....56 D4
Woodroyd Gdns *HORL* RH6 ....56 D5
Woodside *KWD/TDW/WH* KT20 ....24 B3
  LHD/OX KT22 ....8 D2
Woodside Wy *REDH* RH1 ....35 E5
  REDH RH1 ....46 A5
Woodslands *HORL* RH6 ....57 H2
Wood St *REDH* RH1 ....26 C4
Woodville Rd *LHD/OX* KT22 ....3 F5

Woolborough La *REDH* RH1 ....55 F3
Wootton Cl *EPSOM* KT18 ....5 G1
Worcester Rd *REIG* RH2 ....33 G3
Wordsworth Md *REDH* RH1...........35 F2
Worlds End *EPSOM* * KT18 ....5 F1
Worple Rd *LHD/OX* KT22 ....10 B3
Worsted Gn *REDH* RH1 ....26 D4
Wotton Dr *RDKG* RH5 ....38 A5
Wray Common Rd *REIG* RH2 ....34 A3
Wrayfield Av *REIG* RH2.................34 A3
Wraylands Dr *REIG* RH2................34 B2
Wray La *REIG* RH2 ....25 E5
Wraymead Pl *REIG* * RH2 ....33 H3
Wray Mill Pk *REIG* RH2 ....34 B2
Wray Park Rd *REIG* RH2...............33 H3
Wyecliffe Gdns *REDH* RH1 ....26 C5
Wysemead *HORL* RH6 ....57 G2

Z

Zig Zag Rd *RDKG* RH5 2

Y

Yardley Cl *REIG* RH2.....................33 H2
Yarm Cl *LHD/OX* KT22 ....10 C3
Yarm Court Rd *LHD/OX* KT22 ....10 C3
Yarm Wy *LHD/OX* KT22 ....10 C3
Yattendon Rd *HORL* RH6 ....57 F3
Yeats Cl *REDH* RH1......................45 E2
Yeoman Wy *REDH* RH1.................46 B4
Yew Tree Bottom Rd *EW* KT17 ....6 C3
Yew Tree Cl *HORL* RH6 ....57 E1
Yew Tree La *REIG* RH2..................33 H1
Yew Tree Rd *DORK* RH4 ....29 E4
Yorke Gdns *REIG* RH2 ....33 G3
Yorke Rd *REIG* RH2......................33 G3
Young St *LHD/OX* KT22 ....9 H4

Index - featured places

Aberdour School
  KWD/TDW/WH KT20........ 7 F3
All Saints CE Infant School
  LHD/OX KT22.................... 3 E4
Archway Theatre
  HORL RH6 .... 57 E4
The Ashcombe School
  DORK RH4 .... 29 F4
Ashtead Clinic
  ASHTD KT21..................... 4 A2
Ashtead Cricket Club
  ASHTD KT21..................... 4 A2
Ashtead Hospital
  ASHTD KT21..................... 4 A5
Astra Business Centre
  REDH RH1 .... 54 A4
Banstead Athletic FC
  KWD/TDW/WH KT20......... 6 C5
Banstead Sports Centre
  KWD/TDW/WH KT20......... 6 C5
Barnett Wood Infant School
  ASHTD KT21..................... 3 H2
Beacon School
  BNSTD SM7 .... 7 E2
Belfry Shopping Centre
  REDH RH1 .... 34 D3
Betchworth Park Golf Club
  RDKG RH5 .... 30 A5
Bletchingley Golf Club
  REDH RH1 .... 37 F3
Bsocketts Farm Park
  LHD/OX KT22................... 9 H5
Bookham Industrial Estate
  GT/LBKH KT23................. 8 B3
Box Hill Country Park
  KWD/TDW/WH KT20....... 30 A2
Box Hill School
  RDKG RH5 .... 20 B2
Brambletye Junior School
  REDH RH1 .... 46 A1
Bramley School
  KWD/TDW/WH KT20....... 13 E5
Bridge Industrial Estate
  HORL RH6 .... 57 F3
Brockham School
  BRKHM/BTCW RH3........ 41 H1
Brooklands School
  REIG RH2 .... 33 H2
Burghwood Clinic
  BNSTD SM7 .... 7 F1
Burstow Lodge Business Centre
  HORL RH6 .... 57 F5
Burys Court School
  REIG RH2 .... 43 H5

Business Park 5
  LHD/OX KT22................... 3 E5
Chinthurst School
  KWD/TDW/WH KT20....... 13 G3
Chipstead RFC
  COUL/CHIP CR5.............. 15 H1
City of London
  Freemans School
  ASHTD KT21..................... 4 D4
Court Lodge County
  First School
  HORL RH6 .... 56 D3
Crouch Industrial Estate
  LHD/OX KT22................... 3 E4
The Dawnay County
  Primary School
  GT/LBKH KT23............... 18 C1
Denbies Wine Estate
  RDKG RH5 .... 29 F2
Donyngs Recreation Centre
  REDH RH1 .... 34 C3
Doods Brow School
  REDH RH1 .... 36 B3
The Dorking Business Park
  DORK RH4 .... 29 E5
Dorking Cemetery
  DORK RH4 .... 29 G4
Dorking FC
  RDKG RH5 .... 20 C4
Dorking General Hospital
  DORK RH4 .... 40 A2
Dorking Golf Club
  RDKG RH5 .... 40 C2
Dorking Halls
  DORK RH4 .... 29 G5
Dorking Lawn Tennis &
  Squash Club
  DORK RH4 .... 40 A3
Dorking Museum
  DORK RH4 .... 29 G5
Dorking RFC
  BRKHM/BTCW RH3........ 30 D4
Dorking Swimming &
  Sports Centre
  DORK RH4 .... 29 G5
Dovers Green School
  REIG RH2 .... 45 E3
Downsend School
  LHD/OX KT22................... 3 H5
Downsend School -
  Ashtead Lodge
  ASHTD KT21..................... 4 A3
Dunottar School
  REIG RH2 .... 34 B5

Earlswood Infant School
  REDH RH1 .... 35 E5
Earlswood Mosque
  REDH RH1 .... 45 H1
East Surrey College
  REDH RH1 .... 26 A5
  REDH RH1 .... 35 E1
East Surrey Hospital
  REDH RH1 .... 46 B3
Eastwick Infant School
  GT/LBKH KT23................. 8 D4
Eastwick Junior School
  GT/LBKH KT23................. 8 D4
Epsom Cemetery
  EPSOM KT18................... 5 G1
Epsom Downs Racecourse
  EPSOM KT18................... 6 A3
Fairfield Medical Centre
  GT/LBKH KT23............... 18 D1
Fetcham Social & Sports Club
  LHD/OX KT22................... 9 G1
Fetcham Village Infant School
  LHD/OX KT22................... 9 F2
Fontigarry Farm Business Park
  REIG RH2 .... 53 E3
Furzefield Primary School
  REDH RH1 .... 26 D3
Gatton Park Business Centre
  REDH RH1 .... 26 B5
Gatwick Park Hospital
  HORL RH6 .... 56 C4
Great Bookham County
  Infant School
  GT/LBKH KT23............... 18 C1
Greville Primary School
  ASHTD KT21..................... 4 B2
Happy Valley Golf Club
  CTHM CR3 .... 17 H3
Havenbury Industrial Estate
  DORK RH4 .... 29 E5
The Hawthorns Pre-prep School
  REDH RH1 .... 36 D1
Heath Business Centre
  REDH RH1 .... 54 B4
Heathcote Medical Centre
  KWD/TDW/WH KT20....... 13 H2
Hockley Industrial Centre
  REDH RH1 .... 34 D5
Holmesdale School
  REIG RH2 .... 33 H2
Holmethorpe Industrial Estate
  REDH RH1 .... 35 F1
Horley Anderson Sports Centre
  HORL RH6 .... 56 C3

Horley Health Centre
  HORL RH6 5
Howard of Effingham School
  EHSLY KT24................... 1
Hyland Business Centre
  REDH RH1 3
Kingsfield Business Centre
  REDH RH1 3
Kingswood Golf Club
  KWD/TDW/WH KT20....... 1
Kingswood Primary School
  KWD/TDW/WH KT20....... 2
Langshott County Infant School
  HORL RH6 5
Lawn Tennis Club
  HORL RH6 5
  REDH RH1 3
Leatherhead Business Park
  LHD/OX KT22...................
Leatherhead Clinic
  LHD/OX KT22................... 1
Leatherhead Cricket Club
  LHD/OX KT22................... 1
Leatherhead FC
  LHD/OX KT22................... 1
Leatherhead Golf Club
  LHD/OX KT22................... 1
Leatherhead Hospital
  LHD/OX KT22................... 1
Leatherhead Industrial Estate
  LHD/OX KT22................... 1
Leatherhead Institute
  LHD/OX KT22................... 1
Leatherhead Leisure Centre &
  Water Park
  LHD/OX KT22................... 1
Leatherhead Museum
  LHD/OX KT22................... 1
Leigh Primary School
  REIG RH2 4
Manor House School
  EHSLY KT24................... 1
Meath Green County
  Infant School
  HORL RH6 5
Meath Green Junior School
  HORL RH6 5
Merland Rise Primary School
  KWD/TDW/WH KT20.......
Merstham Primary School
  REDH RH1 2
Micklefield School
  REIG RH2 3
Mole Business Park
  LHD/OX KT22................... 1